A Call to Order

A Call to Order

Church Governance:
A Historical, Legal,
and Practical Perspective

Larry L. Crain

ISBN: 979-8-218-13130-2

Cover design by LACreative
Front cover photo of the Altar of the Cistercian abbey of Thonoret in
    the Var in France, copyright © Raphael Navarro, acquired
    through Dreamstime.com
Back cover author photo by Jordan Roepke Photography, LLC
Page layout by Win-Win Words LLC

Printed in the United States of America

To Florence, whose steadfast love and devotion have been a call to order in my life as constant as the northern star.

Contents

Prologue

C HURCHES OCCUPY A UNIQUE PLACE in our legal landscape. Church conflicts—whether internal or risen from an external threat—pose perplexing legal challenges that require legal guidance and expertise from someone trained in ecclesiastical and constitutional law. The impetus for this book is the same that prompted the formation of Church Law Institute. The Institute is dedicated to providing churches with the means to flourish and persevere in a post-modern, post-Christendom American culture that seeks to marginalize and neutralize churches committed to a Scripture-based, evangelical worldview. Note that the Institute's assistance is available to any church regardless of its denominational background or particular form of church polity.

During the several decades that I have represented churches, pastors, and church ministries, I have witnessed trials and struggles that occur when churches are attacked from within, causing some aspect of their governance to fail. Some of their stories are told and discussed in this book. Internal strife left unchecked often leads to dissension and church splits that can tear at the foundation of the church's ability to serve as salt and light. If not dealt with effectively and biblically, such internal divisions can, and often do, lead to schisms with devastating consequences for the church. Church Law Institute is fulfilling a vital role by providing churches and church leaders with sound legal, proactive approaches designed to fend off destructive forces before they take root in the church.

Church Law Institute is a national, nonprofit legal and educational ministry that provides sound legal guidance and biblical conciliation services to churches and church leaders to help those churches flourish. Its primary goal is to free the church from legal entanglements. This is so that church's leadership may devote time and resources toward fulfilling their scriptural mission to spread the Gospel of the Lord Jesus Christ. The Institute's attorneys and staff are committed to equipping churches with a comprehensive legal resource of counsel, education, conflict resolution, and advice and referral on legal issues impacting all aspects of church ministry. To learn more about its mission, purpose, and the services it provides, visit http://www.churchlawinstitute.com.

— **Larry L. Crain**
Founder and Senior Counsel, Church Law Institute

Acknowledgments

To Brian Schuette, for his significant contribution as a co-founder of Church Law Institute, and as pioneer and founder of Acts 6 Project, a vital legal ministry and resource for churches.: https://www.acts6project.com

To Joshua Hershberger, for his vision and work with The Good Citizen Project, a ministry dedicated to equipping Christians to be gospel-centered citizens. https://www.goodcitizen.us

Introduction

INTERNAL DISSENSION IN A CHURCH can be a destructive force regardless of the form of ecclesiastical polity—be it episcopal,
presbyterian, or congregational. We know this from centuries of
church schisms and denominational splits. Church conflict knows
no denominational lines. Despite this historical backdrop of
church factionalism, sadly, many church leadership bodies give
more time and attention to the color of the sanctuary carpet than
to the need for organizational fitness. When it comes to formula-
ting the constitution and bylaws of the church—which define the
DNA of the church body—many churches approach this with ca-
sual indifference. They either blindly adopt the same boilerplate
bylaws handed down generationally by their denomination or,
worse yet, they refer to Scripture as their only source for resolving
issues of internal disagreement.

Sound church governance involves far more than merely
adopting a comprehensive set of church bylaws, although this is
an essential first step. Such governance at its core adheres to a
consistent commitment to a model of scriptural leadership roles
and respect for division of responsibility for those in leadership
positions. It begins with the selection of individuals who possess

character qualifications of fortitude, spiritual maturity, and humility. Church leaders should devote themselves to careful planning in anticipation of the many types of conflicts before they arise. When those conflicts occur, as inevitably they will, church leaders must be able and prepared to make tough calls and stand by them.

The study of church governance is as broad and encompassing as church history itself. The first act of church government was the apostles' appointment of Matthias to replace Judas as one of their body of twelve. Churches of all denominations throughout the millennia have been challenged to adopt and adhere to various forms of self-governance. This process balances the need for consistent, biblical, and sound spiritual leadership with the foibles of human frailty and the need for internal accountability.

Doctors undergo intensive training—practicums, internships, and residencies—before being entrusted with the care of a patient. Law schools also require law students to undergo moot court training to gain an understanding of how cases are actually adjudicated in courts. By contrast, pastors today serve in complex roles, much like CEOs. They must provide more than spiritual guidance to their congregations. Pastors are expected to lead their church, which means making difficult decisions, often in the face of internal dissension, that risk alienating some segment of the congregation.

Very few seminaries offer courses in church government or training to prepare clergy for this daunting role. Such needs for practical guidance for future church leaders is perhaps best summarized by Dr. Steven B. Cowan:

> I am not sure that I can prove that this is how most Christians approach such issues, but my own personal experience provides me with much anecdotal evidence. I never recall, for example, ever hearing any discussions of biblical teaching on

Introduction

church government as I grew up among Southern Baptists (though there was the occasional accusation that Presbyterians and Methodists had it all wrong). And even when I went to seminary (a large Southern Baptist seminary), neither my classes in systematic theology nor in pastoral ministry offered so much as one lecture on forms of church government and the rationale that we Baptists have for doing things our way. I do not think that my experience is unique.[1]

One impetus for this book is the seeming lack of educational or literary works on church governance. As Cowan points out, there is a need for a fresh, critical examination of this topic that challenges those in leadership in Christian ministry to think outside the mold:

> Of course, the major systematic theologies published recently still contain the required chapter on church government for the sake of completeness. And denominational presses no doubt publish books and pamphlets on such ecclesiological issues for their constituencies. Yet, despite the historical and practical significance of church government for church unity, there has been a dearth of books and articles written in venues and for audiences designed to engender serious dialogue among dissenting parties. And my own experience as a pastor and teacher tells me that the average evangelical Christian, no less than the scholar, has not so much as considered that "the way we do things in church" might actually be wrong.[2]

In *A Call to Order*, we begin with some actual cases involving church conflict that led to courtroom battles.

---

[1] Steven B. Cowan, *Who Runs the Church?: 4 Views on Church Government* (Grand Rapids, MI: Zondervan, 2009), 7–8. Dr. Cowan presents a forum for enlightening discussion on all three recognized forms of church government: episcopal, presbyterian, and congregational (both single elder-led and multiple elder-led) and, for each, allows commentary from renowned theologians from each of these three ecclesiastical backgrounds.

[2] Cowan, *Who Runs the Church?*, 9.

We will also look at some of the history of evolving church polity, tracing its early beginnings to the Book of Acts and the apostolic age (sometimes called "patristic" age) when local apostle-planted churches were spread across Asia Minor, Judea, and the Roman Empire. After Constantine, the Great Schism, and the later Protestant Reformation, notions of church governance continued to evolve through the Calvinist, Presbyterian, and Anabaptist movements. Wesleyan revivalists sparked even further reforms to church governance approaches.

It might be helpful here to establish a working definition of *polity*. Once, when I was in court representing one church in a bitter church split case, the judge commented that he had to look up this term *polity* while reading the legal briefs; he was unfamiliar with its use in the context of a church. *Church polity*, as used in this book, refers to "the organization or governmental structure of a local church or fellowship of churches."[3] It is how a church has decided it will govern itself. Generally, as we shall see, church polity may be classified in three recognized forms: hierarchical, presbyterian, and congregational.

While a brief historical perspective is useful in gaining an understanding of how various models of church governance have evolved since the book of Acts, our emphasis shall be on the autonomous, congregational form. Our reasons for giving closer examination to the congregational church are:

(1) local, independent churches do not look to an outside ecclesiastical body for control or ownership of church property, nor do they look to a higher judicative assembly for appeals of controversies within the church;

(2) autonomous churches all fall within a continuum of congregational autonomy, shaped on one end by the degree to which

---

[3] Millard J. Erickson, "Polity," in *Concise Dictionary of Christian Theology*, rev. ed. (Wheaton, IL: Crossway Books, 2001).

they delegate leadership to a senior pastor or overseer, board of elders, and deacons, and on the opposite extreme by what degree final decision-making rests solely in the vote of the congregation (hyper-congregationalism); and,

(3) congregational church government can be fraught with opportunities for deadlock between rival factions vying for authority. Without careful planning, these deadlocks can often cripple or destroy the local ministry. That's why these churches appear to be most in need of practical legal guidance when it comes to a church government resource. It is our hope at Church Law Institute that the principles discussed here will benefit churches and serve to better equip them to chart a course to more effective church leadership and self-governance.

Finally, as should be apparent to anyone trained in ecclesiology and in possession of seminary degrees, I write from the perspective of a constitutional lawyer who has dedicated much of his practice advocating for religious liberty and the defense of the church. I am also a lawyer who is more advocate than apologist. I take solace in the fact that almost two-thirds of the New Testament was also written by a lawyer—Paul.

A Call to Order

1

A Tale of Two Rivers

It was the best of times, it was the worst of times, it was the age of wisdom, it was the age of foolishness, it was the epoch of belief, it was the epoch of incredulity, it was the season of Light, it was the season of Darkness . . ." [4]

TWO RIVERS BAPTIST CHURCH was by all modern-day accounts a successful, vibrant, growing congregational church. In its "best of times," it served as a beacon of evangelical teaching and ministry in Nashville, Tennessee, for more than three generations, eventually boasting of almost seven thousand members and a vast, global missionary outreach. The church was blessed with an exceptionally gifted pastoral staff and leadership. It was a "relevant" church that did not shy away from controversial moral and political issues of the day. It was often in the national headlines serving as a frequent platform for some of the country's most influential leaders who spoke at rallies on conservative and family topics. In 2006, it hosted a pre-election "Stand for the Family" rally sponsored by Focus on the Family Action, featuring such

---

[4] Charles Dickens, *A Tale of Two Cities*, 1859), Ch. 1.

influential leaders such as Dr. James Dobson and Dr. Richard Land. In 2005 Two Rivers hosted "Justice Sunday II," a rally highlighting court rulings on such issues as abortion and Ten Commandments displays. Dobson also spoke at the event, which was held three weeks before the confirmation hearing of now-Supreme Court Chief Justice John Roberts. Also, in 2005, *Hardball with Chris Matthews* hosted a program at the church focusing on religion's role in politics.

The "worst of times" for the church culminated in a disastrous collapse, with events reminiscent of C. S. Lewis's *Screwtape Letters*.[5] The budding conflict began with the defiance of one dissident church trustee who began lashing out at the pastor and church leadership, hurling unfounded accusations of authoritarianism and church mismanagement. Dr. Jerry Sutton—a well-respected pastor who had selflessly served the Two Rivers congregation for twenty-two years, sought conciliation and offered to meet with the trustee and address his concerns. Some of the church deacons and others on staff at first downplayed the significance of such far-flung allegations. They knew that the source of these charges was a lone individual who had a history of divisiveness at earlier churches he had attended. Little did they realize, though, the nature of the flame being kindled by these reckless and defaming remarks, or the proverbial cancer that would metastasize, leading ultimately to the church's destruction and demise.

On September 14, 2007, a small, dissenting faction of individuals seized upon the church trustee's attacks. Disgruntled over the church's "new contemporary style worship service," they

---

[5] C. S. Lewis, William Dendy, and R. B. Green. *The Screwtape Letters* (London: G. Bles, 1952). In fact, some years following the church breakup, Dr. Jerry Sutton published a book *Lectures from the Gates of Hell* (Kindle, 2016), which borrows from the allegories in C. S. Lewis's *Screwtape Letters*.

disregarded Paul's admonition in I Cor. 6 and filed a lawsuit in the Chancery Court of Davidson County, Tennessee, against the church, its senior pastor, executive pastor, associate pastor, chairman of the deacons, church financial secretary, and church clerk.[6] The lawsuit accused all of these church leaders of acting in bad faith in the management of the church finances and demanded that the church pay them damages and attorney's fees. The suit also requested that the court "order the removal of Jerry Sutton as Senior pastor and the other Defendants as officers, directors, and overseers of Two Rivers for their unlawful actions."[7]

We represented Two Rivers Church, Pastor Sutton, and the other church leaders during three long years of this fiercely contested litigation eventually reaching the Tennessee Court of Appeals.[8] The case became a local media sensation and dominated headlines throughout the course of the legal proceedings. Each hearing in court was conducted before a standing-room-only assembly of spectators and journalists.[9]

---

[6] 1 Cor. 6:1-6: "If any of you has a dispute with another, do you dare to take it before the ungodly for judgment instead of before the Lord's people? Or do you not know that the Lord's people will judge the world? And if you are to judge the world, are you not competent to judge trivial cases? Do you not know that we will judge angels? How much more the things of this life. Therefore, if you have disputes about such matters, do you ask for a ruling from those whose way of life is scorned in the church? I say this to shame you. Is it possible that there is nobody among you wise enough to judge a dispute between believers? But instead, one brother takes another to court—and this in front of unbelievers."

[7] *Two Rivers Church, et al v. Sutton, et al.*, Chancery Court of Davidson County, Tennessee, Case No. 07-2088-I, Complaint at ¶ 33.F. The Plaintiffs' allegations in the lawsuit of financial mismanagement were facially spurious. Two Rivers had undergone an audit by an independent accounting firm each of the previous five years.

[8] *Two Rivers v. Sutton*, No. M2008-01730-COA-R3-CV, 2010 WL 2025444 (Tenn.Crt.App. May 20, 2010).

[9] "Welcome to Chancery Court Part I. This is by far the largest number of people who have been in Part I courtroom since I was appointed in October

The church and its pastor leaders and deacons won on every legal and constitutional issue presented in the lawsuit and ultimately prevailed at the appellate level. One of the core issues presented was the extent to which the civil court had jurisdiction to adjudicate matters intricately tied to church governance. From its earliest pleadings, the case centered around what is called the "ecclesiastical abstention doctrine." This doctrine, discussed in greater detail in chapter 6, essentially means that civil courts are not competent to decide matters relating to the doctrinal teachings or internal governing practices of the church. The disgruntled faction expressly sought in their lawsuit to remove the sitting pastor and church leaders, a transparent attempt to impose a court-ordered takeover of the church. Fortunately, the court saw through this and refused to intervene in such a quintessential role of church government.

Throughout the lawsuit, Pastor Sutton and the leadership sought to keep church membership informed of the status of the proceedings. They also pleaded with those who had taken the legal action to repent and return to fellowship within the church. In short, they attempted to lead the church spiritually as they navigated through the most turbulent waters the church had ever encountered.

In a letter to church members, Pastor Sutton and Deacon Carlos Cobos, the church's deacon chairman, appealed to the congregation to decide by churchwide vote whether it was appropriate for the church to impose church discipline on those who had filed the lawsuit:

---

of 2003. . . Persons who are standing inside the courtroom need to step outside the courtroom doors. And you can get as close to the doors as you would like to just so long as you don't get in the way of our security person." Claudia Bonnyman, Chancellor, *Two Rivers Church, et al v. Sutton, et al.*, Chancery Court of Davidson County, Tennessee, Case No. 07-2088-I, (October 26, 2007) Transcript at 1.

Dear Two Rivers Baptist Church Member,

It is with extremely heavy hearts that we write this letter to inform you of actions that will be taking place within our church family in the next two weeks.

A small group of Two Rivers Baptist Church members have continued to practice behaviors that are not consistent with the Word of God or the Church Covenant. On January 8, 2008, the Deacons wrote a letter to the church members who signed a lawsuit against the church and nine church leaders. The purpose of the letter was to pursue reconciliation with these members, to ask them to stop their divisive activities, and to request that they apologize to the church. To further encourage reconciliation, the Deacons met privately with many of these individuals in their homes and listened to their concerns. Elected church leaders also met several times in group sessions with some of these members to answer any questions they had regarding the finances of the church. Despite the multiple meetings and the many hours spent listening to and responding to these individuals' concerns, a public rebuke, and a call to our church body for a time of fasting and prayer, repentance and reconciliation have not occurred.[10]

Despite the multiple meetings and the many hours spent listening to and responding to these individuals' concerns, a public rebuke, and a call to our church body for a time of fasting and prayer, repentance and reconciliation had not occurred.

The church leadership called for a vote of the church membership to "dismiss" seventy-one individuals who had allied with the dissenting church trustee and brought the lawsuit. The following notice was included in the letter to the church membership:

---

[10] Letter from Dr. Jerry Sutton and Carlos Cobos to membership of Two Rivers Baptist Church, April 23, 2008.

Because these deliberate and sinful actions on the part of each Plaintiff have damaged the church's witness and welfare, the Deacon Officers recommend to the church to vote to dismiss the 71 Plaintiffs currently on the membership rolls of Two Rivers Baptist Church. This vote will take place at a special called business meeting at 12:15 P.M. on Sunday, May 4, 2008. There will be no discussion at this meeting. Discussion preceding the vote will be held on Thursday, May 1, 2008, from 6:30 P.M. to 8:00 P.M.

We continue to plead with each individual Plaintiff, for the sake of the Kingdom and that of Two Rivers Baptist Church, to recognize their sin, to repent, and to join the rest of the Two Rivers body as we move ahead. Because the plaintiffs have aligned themselves as a group, our church will vote on them as a group. At the same time, they are individuals and can separate themselves from the group. If a Plaintiff chooses to repent any time prior to May 4, he or she may contact the church office to arrange a private meeting with two Deacons. Those Plaintiffs who choose repentance must remove themselves from the lawsuit and pledge not to be a part of an appeal or any future lawsuits, and to apologize for their actions. For those Plaintiffs who choose to repent, the church family will forgive (Luke 17:3–4, Ephesians 4:32, Colossians 3:12–13) and they will not be included in the vote to be dismissed as members.

Following a voting irregularity that required a second ballot be cast, the church body voted overwhelmingly in favor of dismissing all seventy-one of the individuals who filed the lawsuit as members of Two Rivers Baptist Church. None of the seventy-one dissenting members accepted the church's offer to simply repent and be restored to fellowship. To make matters worse, the congregation's decision to excise this faction from the church did not deter the dissenters from continuing on their determined course to destroy the church. Several of them also joined in mounting a vicious social media campaign attacking and libeling Dr. Sutton and his family.

With church attendance dropping rapidly, Dr. Jerry Sutton on August 3, 2008, accepted a retirement offer from Two Rivers Baptist Church, ending his twenty-two-year tenure as its pastor. By then, attendance had dwindled to 575, down from more than three times that number each Sunday prior to the lawsuit. Unable to sustain the economic burden of maintaining its 37.5-acre campus any longer, the church, under the leadership of its new pastor, Len Taylor, sold its property to the local Catholic diocese. The fledgling congregation relocated outside of Nashville to Mt. Juliet, Tennessee, and changed its name to "The Fellowship at Two Rivers." A religious-operated counseling center now stands in the place of what was once a thriving megachurch.

The Two Rivers case became in many ways a textbook example of what can happen in church litigation cases when a small faction within the church is bent on imposing its will on the majority.[11] While the church and its leadership ultimately prevailed on all legal issues, the church and its pastor became the target of liberal media slants and attacks. Virtually all of the news coverage negatively portrayed the pastor and leaders of Two Rivers and

---

[11] In addition to I Cor. 6, the actions of this minority faction that brought this lawsuit and the specific allegations leveled against the pastor and church leaders violated other clear scriptural injunctions:

1) Lev. 19:16, 1 Cor. 5:11, and 1 Tim. 5:19 by publicly accusing our Pastor of serious legal, ethical and moral failures with no credible evidence to substantiate their claims;

2) Violating Prov. 6:16-19 and Gal. 5:20 by causing division and dissension within our body;

3) Violating Heb. 13:17 in their defiance of elected spiritual authority.

4) Violating several tenets of the Two Rivers Baptist Church Covenant and the Scripture on which it is based, including serving and loving one another, having a Spirit of unity, being Christ-like, and not talking negatively about each other. (See John 13:14, 13:34; Rom. 15:5; 1 Cor. 1:10; 1 Pet. 2:21; and Jas. 4:11).

seized upon every opportunity to stir up the controversy. Pastor Sutton, who just prior to the lawsuit had been a national candidate in 2006 for the presidency of the Baptist Southern Convention, was viciously assailed by the media across the country. Having stood as a beacon of evangelism for generations, the church became marred with twisted half-truths. Church attendance plummeted. False rumors of impropriety swirled in the Nashville community, and within the walls of the church. One elderly woman raised a fist during one evening church service and shouted at the pastor, "Nazi!"

As I sat in the service that evening, witnessing the collapse of a great church and once powerful ministry, I remember saying to myself, *This simply should not be.* Surely, there must be a better way to protect churches against such a calamity than going to battle in court. This tragedy became the primary impetus for the creation of Church Law Institute.

2

No Governing Documents:
A Lesson in Church Anarchy

T HE CHURCH OF THE FIRST BORN is a pastor-elder-led congregational church in Tennessee that was founded in 1933
by an itinerant, country minister named Prator Donald "P. D."
Hardin. The church occupies more than seventy-five acres of
land, and includes a church school called Dayspring Academy,
a Christian camp, and two sanctuaries—one in White House,
Tennessee, and another in Hartsville, Tennessee, located in separate counties. During the first seventy-plus years of its existence, the Church of the First Born thrived under the leadership
of P. D. Hardin, who died in 1983, and then under his successor,
Bob Hardin, who passed away in 2008.[12] The church was a "single-elder led church" during this time. That meant final authority regarding all spiritual matters was vested at all times in
the elder-overseer of the church. His recommendations were
also regarded as final on financial matters.

The Church of the First Born never adopted church bylaws.

Bob Hardin was the last elder-overseer of the church. When
Hardin passed in 2008, a number of deacons who had begun wor-

---

[12] According to one estimate, by the time of Bob Hardin's death, the church
had amassed in excess of $14 million of real property.

9

shipping at the church's Hartsville location tried to seize control over all aspects of the church. They also attempted to oust the pastor of the larger of the two sanctuaries, the one in White House. This dissenting group also took advantage of Bob Hardin's death as an opportunity to challenge the longstanding doctrinal teachings of the church, including the church's tenets regarding the sacrament of baptism. In addition, they challenged the church's longstanding commitment to operating a church school.

Just as Shakespeare wrote in *Hamlet* ("[A]nd it must follow, as night follows day"),[13] the church split into two factions. Each vied for control over the church's vast properties and, more importantly, for the right to control the church's destiny.

The dissenting deacons promptly filed a lawsuit in the Chancery Court of Robertson County, Tennessee (where the White House campus was located). They sued to oust the pastor of the larger White House congregation and two of its deacons, with the dissidents claiming they represented the "true church." Meanwhile, the pastor of the White House congregation still enjoyed the virtual unanimous support of the White House congregation, which far outnumbered the Hartsville congregation. To further compound and complicate the case, the Dayspring Academy was, from its founding, regarded as an integral and inseparable ministry of the church. This school, located on the White House campus, was governed by its own board of directors, all of whom were faithful followers of the White House pastor.

As with most church lawsuits, this dissenting faction, consisting of the three dissenting deacons as well as six senior members and trustees, claimed that by representing the "true church" they had the exclusive right to control all of the church's property, both in White House and Hartsville. [14]

---

[13] Act 1, Scene 3 of Shakespeare's play, *Hamlet*.

[14] Such lawsuits are typically called actions to "quiet title" and arise when

In order to protect the church proper and to preserve its ability to worship as it had done over the seventy-plus years of its existence, the pastor and deacons at the White House congregation were forced to file a countersuit in Robertson County. They also filed a separate lawsuit in Trousdale County, Tennessee (where the Hartsville campus was located), seeking to "quiet title" to this property. This started one of the longest and most protracted and expensive cases involving internal church conflict in Tennessee history.

A central issue in the Church of the First Born case was which body within the church had the authority to decide matters involving the real property (the land and buildings) of the church. In other words, who within the church had the final say on whether to purchase or sell church land? Is it the elder-overseer? Is it the congregation? Is it the board of deacons? And, if it is the elder-overseer, what happens when the ruling elder-overseer dies without appointing his successor, as was the case when Pastor Bob Hardin passed away? With no bylaws in place to decide this issue, the church was adrift on the sea of uncertainty, and ultimately forced to litigate this issue.

One faction in the case argued that the board of deacons became the final decision-making authority on all matters, both temporal and spiritual. But they could not point to any governing document to support their contention. Over its seventy-year history, the church had made decisions on property issues in a variety of ways, some with deacon board approval, and others by a churchwide vote by the congregation. At other times, property decisions involved a combination of both ways. With no church bylaws in place, the courts in both cases were left with no guidepost or established practice on which to make a "neutral" decision

---

two or more competing groups each claim the right of exclusive control over real property.

as to which faction constituted the "true church" or which group had final decision-making authority when it came to church property matters.

Over the course of eleven years of bitter, hard-fought litigation, the church and those named in the lawsuits spent more than two million dollars in legal costs. Conflicting decisions were issued in both county courts over whether the Church of the First Born was a congregational church or a form of hierarchical church. There were multiple appeals to the Tennessee Court of Appeals to try and untangle what had become convoluted trial court proceedings. At one point, the trial judge commented disdainfully that his chambers looked "like someone had dumped a pick-up truck full of pleadings" pertaining to the case. He later described the case as "a divorce on steroids."

Meanwhile, the church lay in legal limbo in a forced *détente*, its ability to utilize its properties or pursue long-term ministry goals remained stymied. Far more important than the property side of the case, the lawsuits had a stranglehold on the church's ability to flourish and grow. Much like the Two Rivers Church, the bright beacon of light it had been to its surrounding community was dimmed by a dark cloud of litigation. Church resources, and the time and energy of the pastor and other church leaders, were tied up in multiple depositions, court hearings, futile mediation conferences, briefings with their legal counsel, and other distractions that go along with a lawsuit. Even after a week-long trial, issues remained unresolved, thus requiring additional appeals with no final resolution in sight.

The lesson to be learned from the Church of the First Born case is that all of this might have been avoided had the church simply adopted a well-crafted, comprehensive set of church bylaws. It is difficult to overstate the importance of internal governing documents for any church, especially congregational churches. They form the DNA of the church and allow for orderly resolution of church conflicts, succession of authority, and, if done properly, serve as a hedge of protection around the church and its members, pastors, and staff.

3

Laying Claim
to the Local Church:
Theft by Implied Trust

"WHAT DO YOU MEAN we don't own our church property? Our church has been worshipping here since before the Civil War. Four generations of church ancestors are buried in our church cemetery, and we have to just hand all our property over?" This is a question one elderly woman put to me during a church meeting and in response to a demand by the parent-church organization. "But we can fight this in court, right?" another gentleman asked with a pained expression. "Our church was built by the sacrifice of its members who gave of their tithes and offerings. What do you mean it doesn't belong to us?"

As bizarre as it sounds, there is a well-established body of law in the U.S. which provides that in the event a local church desires to withdraw from its parent church organization, in most cases, it forfeits all its property, both real and personal, to the parent church. This doctrine has come to be referred to as the "implied trust theory." Essentially, this doctrine holds that when a local church joins a hierarchical or connectional church organization, it conveys title to all its property in trust to the parent church. It is a rule of hierarchical deference by civil courts to the decisions of judicial bodies within the parent church; as touched on earlier, courts are barred jurisdictionally from substituting their decisions for that of the higher church body. [15]

All of this sounds rather difficult to comprehend by most people, but it has real ramifications for any local church that finds itself outside the fold on doctrinal or human sexuality positions taken by their denomination. Christianity in the twentieth century was characterized by an accelerating secularization of Western society. Beginning in the late 1900s, many denominations in the U.S., especially those that did not adhere to the belief of scriptural inerrancy, began to adopt positions that more traditional, conservative Christians found heretical and anti-family. The result has been the rise of interdenominational strife and schisms within many, if not most, of the hierarchical denominations. These include Episcopalian, Anglican, Methodist, Presbyterian, Lutheran, and others.

The advent of gay-lesbian ordination of ministers, approval of same-sex marriage, and the rejection of traditional, biblical notions of the family have sparked smoldering debates over scriptural interpretations and led many local churches to withdraw from their denominations. Thousands of them severed denominational ties, and either established their own congregational church or formed new alliances rejecting this modern shift in cultural norms.

Church schisms occur when a single religious body divides and becomes two or more independent religious bodies, with each claiming a right of self-governance. Religious schisms are not new to the Christian church. Since the days of the apostles, history records show more than fifty major schisms during the Catholic, pre-Reformation era, and hundreds more since the

---

[15] For a good discussion of this doctrine, see "A Multitude of Sins? Constitutional Standards for Legal Resolution of Church Property Disputes in a Time of Escalating Interdenominational Strife," 35 Pepp. L. Rev. 399 (2008).

Protestant Reformation.[16] During the American Civil War (1861–1865), many denominations, including Baptist, Methodist, and Presbyterian, split over the issue of slavery. Following the war, denominational splits continued unabated over the admission of African Americans as members of traditionally white churches.

Competing conceptions of property rights are merely the tip of a church-state iceberg and implicate more than two hundred years of American jurisprudence involving the First Amendment's religion clauses. Schisms in mainline denominations, including most prominently the Episcopal Church, the Presbyterian Church (United States of America [PC (USA)]), and the United Methodist Church have been plagued by internal strife over theological shifts for decades. Civil courts are all too frequently called on to resolve disputes over who owns property that departing congregations had been using.

Because of the myriad complex issues presented in intrachurch litigation, courts, churches, and their attorneys must be informed about the constitutional standards involved. Likewise, these parties must be knowledgeable about the ways in which states have adopted, adapted, and applied these constitutional standards, and they must be aware where this area of the law might be headed as America's mainline denominations continue to struggle with contrasting visions of self-identity.

Methodist Churches: The Cost of Church Autonomy

Attorneys with Church Law Institute have been called into dozens of cases to represent local Methodist congregations desiring to disaffiliate from the United Methodist Conference over its

---

[16] The Great Schism or Schism of 1054 was the break of communion that occurred in the eleventh century between the Catholic Church and Eastern Orthodox Church.

denominational deviation from its original position on issues of human sexuality and the family. The following is a look at two of these churches and their struggle for church autonomy.

The Salem Church

The Salem Methodist Church is a congregational church near Cookeville, Tennessee, that was founded in 1820. As small, Methodist churches go, Salem was typical in its form of worship tracing its doctrinal roots to the John Wesleyan movement. In 1735, John Wesley and his brother, Charles, migrated from England to the Georgia Colony and began to preach the Gospel to the Native American tribes. They eventually returned to England and formulated what became the Wesleyan doctrines of Methodism. This involved preaching salvation by faith alone, and teaching that outward holiness was a product of faith.

Following the American Revolution in the late eighteenth century, several Anglican clergy returned to England. Impressed by the teachings of John Wesley, many became his followers and disciples. Two of them, Thomas Coke and Francis Asbury, were sent by Wesley to America where they founded the Methodist Episcopal Church. This movement sparked formation of the single largest denomination in America during the nineteenth century.

In 1785, the Methodist Episcopal Church published the first version of *The Book of Discipline,* which is its bible (with a lowercased "b") containing the constitution, doctrine, doctrinal statements, general rules of church governance, and various organizational rules of the Methodist Church. Unquestionably, *The Book of Discipline* establishes a very ordered hierarchical structure built around the concept of the Conference. The word *Conference*, as described in this governing church document, refers to an annual gathering of church leaders—called an "Annual Conference"—who meet to debate church policies and financial affairs. Various local "Districts," similar to dioceses, with each having a district superintendent, are formed within these Annual Conferences. Each year these Annual Conferences also send delegates to a "General Conference," which is the national tip of the Methodist hierarchy and the highest decision-making body in the church.

Well into the 1900s, Methodist Churches continued to flourish throughout the U.S., and, in 1968, many joined to form what became the United Methodist Church. The General Conference has been the subject of much controversy over the rift between Annual Conferences and church leaders regarding gay and lesbian ordination and same-sex marriage. This concern on the part of local churches over the denomination's shift from traditional views of marriage and human sexuality led the Salem Methodist Church to reach out to Church Law Institute for help in severing its ties with the United Methodist Church.

"We just cannot agree as a church with the direction the denomination seems to be headed, Mr. Crain. Would you be willing to come speak to our members about what we can do to pull out of the Conference?"

At the time, the United Methodist Church was embroiled in a national debate over this same issue. One retired Methodist bishop, Nashville's Melvin Talbert, faced church discipline over officiating the marriage of two men in Alabama. Bishop Talbert garnered several allies within the United Methodist Church, but the handwriting was on the wall, and a church schism seemed inevitable.

Like many of its sister churches, the Salem Methodist Church in the late 1960s had joined the United Methodist Church and became a member church in the Annual Conference in Tennessee. Little did its members realize at the time the consequences of joining this union of churches.

The Book of Discipline provides that each local church is responsible for conducting its affairs in strict accordance with this governing document. Among the requirements imposed on the local church is that each church must provide annual reports to the Conference. These reports must contain information about the church's membership and a financial report describing the land, buildings, and personal property. In addition, it must summarize the church's receipts and expenditures from whatever source derived and for whatever purpose. The Church must pay "apportionments" to the Conference based on its size and income, and it must accept a pastor appointed by the district superintendent.

The Book of Discipline also contains a "trust clause," which provides that all of the church's land, buildings, and funds are held in trust for the benefit of the entire denomination. In other words, even though the church's deed may reflect that the land was conveyed to the local church back in the mid-1880s, by joining the denomination, the church is deemed to have conveyed the land to the United Methodist Conference. While reference to this trust clause is required to be recited in every deed to church property, oftentimes it is not. But even in the absence of any such provision in the church's deed, several courts have ruled that the Conference is the beneficiary and rightful owner through an "implied trust" of all property owned by the local church.

As one may expect, this "implied trust" doctrine has tremendous significance for local congregations, and many of them are unaware of the legal consequences of this provision.

From a legal standpoint, the United Methodist Church, through its various Annual Conferences, takes the position that the moment a local church joins the United Methodist Conference, this implied trust is immediately imposed on all local church holdings, and that it becomes the rightful owner of the church's bank accounts, cemeteries, and parsonages, all the way down to the church pews.

Specifically, paragraph 2501 of *The Book of Discipline* provides, in relevant part:

> Requirement of the Trust Clause for All Property- 1. All properties of United Methodist local churches and other United Methodist agencies and institutions are held, in trust, for the benefit of the entire denomination, and ownership and usage of church property is subject to the Discipline since 1797. If reflects the connectional structure of the church by ensuring that the property will be used solely for the purposes consonant with the mission of the entire denomination as set forth in the Discipline. The trust requirement is thus a fundamental expression of United Methodism whereby local churches and other agencies and institutions within the denomination are both held accountable to and benefit from their connection with the entire worldwide Church.

When the Salem Church's lay leaders sent a letter to the District Superintendent advising it that the congregation had voted unanimously to withdraw from the United Methodist Church, to their shock and dismay they received back a Notice to Vacate the Premises and to turn over the church's keys and bank accounts.

Virtually every local Methodist church that has come to Church Law Institute for assistance in exiting the denomination has attested that they were unfamiliar with the legal impact of this provision in *The Book of Discipline*. They were certain that the concept of a binding "implied trust" was never fully explained to their predecessors at the time the church joined the United Methodist Conference decades earlier.

Indeed, there was little occasion for local churches to dwell on the implied trust doctrine until a situation arose requiring them to withdraw their membership in the United Conference; then it became a big issue.

When this legal doctrine was presented to the congregants at Salem Methodist Church, one could hear a pin drop. *Do you mean, the Conference can padlock our doors if we vote to leave as a church? Can they attach our bank accounts and missionary budget? What about our cemetery? Surely, they cannot confiscate the graves of our church ancestors who have been buried there for over a century, right?*

Many of the congregants looked on in disbelief when they were advised that if they wanted out of the Conference, they would have to hire a lawyer to "negotiate" their withdrawal. Unless this process was handled diplomatically, the church stood to forfeit what had taken generations of sacrificial giving to build and maintain.

Salem Church, like many of the other churches that came to Church Law Institute for help on disaffiliation, based their opposition to the "implied trust" doctrine on a simple, seemingly persuasive argument: If the denomination that the church joined has departed from its founding doctrines on such important issues as the scriptural teachings on human sexuality and the Christian family, then it has breached its covenant with the local church. In other words, the denomination has departed from its original teachings, and this should serve to void, or at least render unenforceable, the implied trust theory.

As appealing as this argument sounds on its surface, the problem oftentimes is that, once again, a civil court cannot wade into controversies over religious doctrine. It is forbidden to decide such matters, and constitutionally constrained from doing so. Instead, under the so-called ecclesiastical abstention doctrine, courts must defer to decision-making bodies within a church, and cannot substitute their judgments as a civil court for those of such church bodies. Based on this legal doctrine, several courts have enforced the implied trust doctrine in favor of the

Annual Conference or General Conference, and ruled against local churches. Essentially, courts have held that the local church knew, or should have known, when it joined the denomination that these were the terms of membership.

There is some good news. In every single case in which a local Methodist church has come to Church Law Institute for assistance, the church was ultimately permitted to withdraw from the United Methodist Conference, and was able to purchase its freedom and maintain its church property for negligible amounts. In the case of the Salem Methodist Church, it is today a thriving congregational church attracting young new members. Church Law Institute was instrumental in incorporating this church and helping them draft their own church bylaws with safeguards to navigate through future internal church conflicts. New church position statements were also drafted that expressly stated the church's doctrinal position on matters of human sexuality and the traditional and scriptural definition of the Christian family.

4

Early Beginnings:
The Acts of the Apostles

A NY DISCUSSION OF THE ORIGINS of church governance must begin, of course, with the Book of Acts. All modern, biblical-based models of ecclesiastical polity, from the most formal episcopal hierarchy to the autonomous, congregational church, consistently cite some portion of these twenty-eight chapters of scripture as support for their form of church governance.

As Luke opens the curtain on this book, the disciples are looking skyward in wonder at the ascension of Christ. Quickly, though, their attention is drawn back to earth and the need to perform their first important act of church governance—the selection of a successor for Judas Iscariot. This passage provides insight into the proper biblical groundwork laid by them for making such a momentous decision:

> Then they returned to Jerusalem from the mount called Olivet, which is near Jerusalem, a Sabbath day's journey. And when they entered, they went up into the upper room where they were staying: Peter, James, John, and Andrew; Philip and Thomas; Bartholomew and Matthew; James the son of Alphaeus and Simon the Zealot; and Judas the son of James. These all continued in one accord in prayer and supplication,

with the women and Mary the mother of Jesus, and with His brothers. . . .

. . . And they proposed two: Joseph called Barsabas, who was surnamed Justus, and Matthias. And they prayed and said, "You, O Lord, who know the hearts of all, show which of these two You have chosen to take part in this ministry and apostleship from which Judas by transgression fell, what he might go to his own place." And they cast their lots, and the lot fell on Matthias. And he was numbered with the eleven apostles.[17]

Having reconstituted itself as the ruling body of the early church in Jerusalem, the church, in its first three years under apostolic leadership, was punctuated with peril and persecution. From this compact gathering of 120, we are told in Acts 2:41 that this initial assembly exploded in just seven weeks to more than 3,000 by the time of Pentecost. By the time of Peter and John's arrest in Acts 4, the body of believers had grown to more than 5,000 men (women and children are not counted). There was no precedent for governing such a fast-growing congregation, and we are given little insight into the operational structure followed by the early church leadership.

The martyrdom of Stephen had a pronounced impact on the spread of the early church.[18] According to Thom Rainer, this single act of persecution is believed to have led to a propagation of small congregations throughout Asia Minor and elsewhere:

The martyrdom of Stephen (7:54–60) does not reduce the church to a level of frightened ineffectiveness. To the contrary, the persecution that broke out against the disciples scattered

---

[17] Acts 1: 12-14, 23-26. (NKJV). Note, all Scripture references, except where indicated, are from the New King James Version.

[18] Stephen is mentioned as one of seven "deacons" in the early church (Acts 6:5). As we shall see later, the word "deacon" is derived from the Greek word diákonos (διάκονος), which in ancient Greek meant "servant."

the church throughout Judea and Samaria. The defeated church then became the proclaiming church as the dispersion spread the gospel to new areas. God in his sovereignty turned defeat into a larger victory (8:4).

. . . Stephen's death led to the beginning of a massive lay movement which spread the gospel. The "amateur missionaries," those evicted from Jerusalem following Stephen's martyrdom, eventually became the leaders who changed the face of the movement by preaching to the Greeks and initiating the Gentile mission at Antioch.[19]

At the same time the early church was facing fierce external persecution, internal sources of dissension tested the early church leaders.

If the murder of Stephen was an external factor that led to the growth of the church, Luke would have us note that numerous internal problems were also turned into divine victories. One such example is the Ananias and Sapphira incident of Acts 5. In his typical pattern of conflict/surprise/victory, Luke relates what seems to be an overwhelming internal problem: deceit within the fellowship. The surprise factor is the death of the two perpetrators at the hands of God. The victory is noted in a rapid-fire sequence of events: all who heard about the incident were seized with fear (5:11); the "outside world" highly regarded the church (5:11); and "more and more men and women believed in the Lord and were added to their number" (5:14).[20]

During the first seventy years of early church existence, the difficulties faced by newly planted churches in such pagan centers of cultural diversity as Ephesus and Thessalonica were myriad.[21] These seedlings sprang up from messages preached by itinerant

---

[19] Thom S. Rainer, "Church Growth and Evangelism in the Book of Acts," *Criswell Theological Review* 5.1 (1990), 62-64.

[20] Rainer.

[21] Paul's missionary journeys occurred between A.D. 46 and A.D. 62.

apostles who were rarely afforded the luxury of staying in one place long enough to disciple and train church leaders in matters of internal governance. Hence, many of these early churches were left to fend for themselves awaiting the next "epistle." This would redirect their path and instruct them in matters of church discipline as well as the qualifications of those whom they were to appoint to positions of service and leadership in the church.

So much of early church leadership and governance was imparted by example and mirrored in the life of the apostle. However, when physical presence was not possible, a disciple had to be sent to shepherd the newly formed flock.

> I do not write these things to shame you, but as my beloved children I warn you. For though you might have ten thousand instructors in Christ, yet you do not have many fathers; for in Christ Jesus I have begotten you through the gospel. Therefore, I urge you, imitate me. For this reason, I have sent Timothy to you, who is my beloved and faithful son in the Lord, who will remind you of my ways in Christ, as I teach everywhere in every church.[22]

Likewise, these early fledgling churches did not have the benefit of community and association and were truly autonomous to the point of being isolated from other believers. This perhaps explains the lack of uniformity in the form of worship they practiced and the absence of any common accepted leadership structure. Consequently, these early churches were a fertile ground for dissension. Divisions sprung up from within the church in Corinth, for example, regarding which faction was spiritually superior to the others based solely on who had baptized them.[23]

In the next chapter we will see how persecution of the early followers of Christ led to the propagation and spread of churches

---

[22] 1 Cor. 4:14–17.
[23] 1 Cor. 1:11–13.

throughout the formative years of the church. We will also learn how the religious apartheid imposed by emperors such as Nero and Domitian only fueled all the more the wonder of the pagan world at those who were called to be witnesses (from the word *martyr*) for Christ.

5

Governing the Persecuted Church: Jerusalem to Rome

T HE BIRTHPLACE OF THE FIRST ECCLESIASTICAL ASSEMBLY of followers of Christ was Jerusalem. Despite intense persecution
from the Jews and Herod, this earliest of churches was not without a semblance of form and structure. The first council of the
apostles is believed to have occurred in 53 A.D. and was presided
over by James, the brother of Jesus.[24] In the Jerusalem church, all
authority regarding the teachings of Christ, the doctrinal instruction, and church governance was concentrated in the holy family,
represented by James and the twelve apostles, led by Peter, James,
and John, the sons of Zebedee. James would later be recognized
as the bishop or overseer of the church in Jerusalem, and he led
the congregation until his martyrdom.[25]

The explosion in church growth following Pentecost crossed
ethnic, racial, and social barriers that were sacrosanct prior to the
church. Suddenly, the Jewish apostles were confronted with the

---

[24] Acts 15:19–21.

[25] "Now about that time Herod the king stretched forth his hands to vex cer-
tain of the church. And he killed James the brother of John with the sword."
Acts 12:1–2. Note, that the name "Herod" refers to a line of Judean kings.
The one responsible for the death of James and the arrest of Peter is Agrippa
I, the grandson of Herod the Great who presided over Jesus's Hebrew trial.

prospect of leading a congregation of Jews, Samaritans, and Gentiles of a multitude of ethnic backgrounds. It is clear that one of the earliest decisions facing the new church leaders was the question of how to deal with such a culturally diverse group of followers.

> And after they had become silent, James answered, saying, "Men and brethren, listen to me: Simon has declared how God at the first visited the Gentiles to take out of them a people for His name. . .
>
> Therefore I judge that we should not trouble those from among the Gentiles who are turning to God, but that we write to them to abstain from things polluted by idols, from sexual immorality, from things strangled, and from blood.[26]

Note that James used the words "therefore, I *judge*. . ." His word on the subject of church membership and godly standards for Gentiles was final.

In addition to the "bishop," "pastor," or "overseer" role occupied by James and that of "elder" shared by the remaining twelve apostles, in Acts chapter 6 we are told that seven "deacons" or servants were chosen to help in ministering to the church body:

> Now in those days, when the number of the disciples was multiplying, there arose a complaint against the Hebrews by the Hellenists, because their widows were neglected in the daily distribution. Then the twelve summoned the multitude of the disciples and said, "It is not desirable that we should leave the word of God and serve tables. Therefore, brethren, seek out from among you seven men of good reputation, full of the Holy Spirit and wisdom, whom we may appoint over this business; but we will give ourselves continually to prayer and to the ministry of the word. And the saying pleased the whole multitude. And they chose Stephen, a man full of faith and the Holy Spirit, and Philip, Prochorus, Nicanor, Timon,

---

[26] Acts 15:13–21.

Parmenas, and Nicolas, a proselyte from Antioch, whom they set before the apostles; and when they had prayed, they laid hands on them."[27]

From the early chapters of Acts it is clear that among the strengths of the Jerusalem church were (1) brotherly love and unity (Acts 2:43–46; 4:32–37), (2) immediate settlement of internal problems (Acts 5,6,15), (3) involvement of all of the members in the deliberations and resolutions of the problems that arose (Acts 6:1–6; 15:22), (4) courage and devotion which led them to continue teaching even in the face of persecution, and (5) an excellent program of teaching, which edified the disciples and gave the church such great teachers as Stephen, Philip, Barnabas, and Silas. The weaknesses of the Jerusalem church were (1) poverty (Acts 2, 4, 11), (2) lying of Ananias and Sapphira (Acts 5), (3) neglect of widows (Acts 6), (4) persecution (Acts 4, 5, 7, 8), and (5) false teaching (Acts 15).

The conversion of Saul of Tarsus in about 37 A.D. is perhaps the single most revolutionizing event in the growth of the early church. It transformed the church from being a particular group within Judaism centered in Jerusalem to an evangelical mission to Asia Minor and Europe. From the beginning of his evangelistic ministry, Paul's missionary endeavors epitomized what it meant to be an apostle of Christ.[28]

During the period of Paul's three missionary journeys from A.D. 46 to 57, the longest period of time we are told he remained in one location was three years when he preached in Ephesus (Acts 20:31). Most of the time his stay was for only a few months. For example, when he met with the disciples of John the Baptist in Jerusalem, he preached in the synagogue for three months

---

[27] Acts 6:1–5.

[28] An apostle, from the Classical Greek ἀπόστολος (apóstolos), literally means "one who is sent away" as a messenger and ambassador.

(Acts 19:8). He disputed daily in the school of Tyrannus for two years (Acts 19:9–10). We are told that he sent Timothy and Erastus ahead into Macedonia, while he stayed behind in Asia "for a season" (Acts 19:22).

With the spread of the church came new issues of church governance. This is due, in part, to the fact that the apostle who planted the church was forced to be an itinerant leader, often governing by epistle (a letter from a recognized church leader). This is especially true of the church leadership model followed by Paul.[29]

For all of his sojourning, Paul was instrumental in writing the qualifications of church leaders. The church at Ephesus became a sort of prototype for Paul's model for church leadership and governance. Prior to writing 1 Timothy, Paul spent much of his three years in Ephesus training a group of godly men to serve as elders (Acts 18:19; 20:17, 31). As a result of Paul's laboring in the discipleship and training of these church leaders, the Ephesian church became a beacon to other churches of a strategic outreach in a pagan culture and solid leadership.

From Ephesus back to Rome, Paul's final abode, it is estimated that he planted between fourteen and twenty churches.[30] There were a number of Christians already in Rome by the time of Paul's house arrest there in 61 A.D. Paul's letter to the Romans was written to a growing grassroots network of Christians who

---

[29] The other apostles also planted churches throughout other regions of the world: Andrew preached to the Scythians [modern-day Georgia] and Thracians [modern-day Bulgaria], and was crucified at Patrae, a town of Achaia [Greece]; Bartholomew led a missionary journey to Asia; Philip preached in Phrygia and was crucified in Hierapolis during the reign of Domitian; and Thomas preached to the Parthians, Medes, Persians, Hyrcanians, Bactrians, and Margians, and was eventually martyred in what is now modern India.

[30] In Asia-Minor alone, Scripture mentions churches begun by Paul in Ephesus, Smyrna, Pergamum, Thyatira, Sardis, Philadelphia, Laodicea, Colossae, and Hieropolis. Churches were spread throughout Ephesus where believers met in homes.

had begun to thrive in Rome. It is unknown just how or when these early Christians first settled there. It is speculated that following the martyrdom of Stephen and later James in Jerusalem, several hundred Jewish and Gentile believers fled the city to the outer reaches of the Roman empire and to Rome.[31]

As for the other twelve apostles, we know from secular history the geographical area covered by their missionary endeavors, but we can only speculate about the number of churches they started. One thing is true; this fledgling group of ambassadors for Christ sparked a movement that would in a very short time ignite the Roman pagan culture and revolutionize Western civilization.

---

[31] Records from the catacombs indicate that there were at least five synagogues in Rome during the early first century. These synagogues were the early breeding ground from which converts to Christianity emerged. See Peter Richardson, "Augustan-Era Synagogues in Rome," in Judaism and Christianity in First-Century Rome (ed. Karl P. Donfried and Peter Richardson (Grand Rapids, MI: Eerdmans, 1998), 19–29. According to Richardson, there might have been as many as thirteen synagogues that have been identified from Roman inscriptions, but only these five can be assumed to have existed before the arrival of Christianity in Rome.

6

From Constantine
to the Medieval Church

T HE FIRST THREE HUNDRED YEARS of the church's existence was
marked by sporadic and often intense persecution. Beginning with the execution of Paul and later Peter under Nero (circa
62–64 A.D.) followed shortly by the Roman siege of Jerusalem
and the destruction of the Temple, Rome had little tolerance for
any religious sect that refused to bow to Rome and Roman gods.
Yet, remarkably in the midst of this torture and persecution,
Christianity flourished.

Not until the Edict of Milan, issued by emperors Constantine the Great and Licinius in 313 A.D., was Christianity's claim
of exclusive devotion to a risen Savior granted legal recognition.
As small cells of Christian followers were allowed to emerge
from the catacombs into the light of day in Roman culture,
unique challenges in the area of church governance and unity
came with them.

As Professor Anne Yarbrough explains, there was an unlikely
underground base of believers who helped propagate the Gospel
and whose cottage Bible studies allowed Christianity to gain a
solid foothold in early Rome:

> At the beginning of the fourth century, the Roman aristocracy
> was, for the most part, pagan in its religious attitude. By the

end of that century the aristocracy had undergone what Peter Brown has described as a "sea change": its pagan values had become redefined within the context of Christianity. This "drift into respectable Christianity" was the result of the process of socialization in the households of the Roman senatorial class over several generations. Brown suggests that the fourth-century Christianization of the aristocracy was the achievement of those upper-class Roman women who, by continuing to practice their Christian religion in the households of their pagan husbands, established the syncretistic milieu which would influence the religious attitudes of the next generation. But the apparent calm of Brown's anonymous culture-bearers is disturbed by a small group of women whose religious extremism delineates them sharply from their peers. Rejecting wholly the society into which they were born, they fled the cloying Roman atmosphere for the harsh air of the desert. The "respectable Christianity" that Rome was adopting offered them no satisfaction.[32]

The forms of church government that prevailed during the second and third centuries varied greatly and were largely dependent on the individual style of leadership of the bishop or overseer of the local congregation. In Smyrna, under the leadership of Polycarp (a student of the Apostle John) and in Antioch, under Ignatius, the influence of these early church patriarchs was evident. Church structure and government was patterned closely after the teachings of Paul. The writings of these early pre-Nicene apostolic fathers such as St. Clement, Mathetes, Barnabas, St. Papias, St. Justin Martyr, St. Irenaeus, and Tertullian were heavily influential on the early church.[33]

---

[32] Anne Yarbrough, *Christianization in the Fourth Century: The Example of Roman Women. Church History* (1976). 45, pp 149–165. doi:10.2307/3163714.
[33] Tertullian is regarded by many as the father of Latin Christianity (c. A.D. 155–220). He was trained to be a lawyer and chose instead to be ordained as a priest, and he was the first Christian apologist to distill a theology of the Trinity and the teaching of God as "three Persons, one Substance."

The Impact of Constantine and the Legitimization of Christianity

The early church during the third and fourth centuries was faced with two imminent threats: one external—the relentless persecution of Rome, and one internal—the Arian heresy that denied the divinity of Christ.[34] Prior to the fourth-century Nicence Creed, Arianism and other competing beliefs concerning the deity of Christ and the nature of the resurrection were often a source of rifts and division among various churches. Strong pronouncements of heresy were leveled against those who dared challenge some of the early cardinal doctrinal positions. Intrachurch disputes were also commonplace based on disagreements over the proper interpretation of Scripture, and canonical differences regarding which writings should be a part of the canon of Scripture.

In the midst of these threats and doctrinal divisions, an emperor rose to power in Rome whose reign would revolutionize the spread of Christianity and have a radical, unifying impact on church government for centuries to come.[35] In A.D. 313, Constantine (with his co-emperor Licinius) issued the famous Edict of Milan, declaring Christianity to be a legal religion. Christianity had

---

[34] Arianism is a theological teaching that denied the existence of the Trinity, and is attributed to Arius (c. A.D. 250–336), a Christian presbyter in Alexandria, Egypt, concerning the relationship of God the Father to the Son of God, Jesus Christ. Arius asserted that the Son of God was a subordinate entity to God the Father. Arius was deemed a heretic by the Ecumenical First Council of Nicaea of 325, but later exonerated in 335 at the regional First Synod of Tyre. The Roman Emperors Constantius II (A.D. 337–361) and Valens A.D. (364–378) ascribed to the Arianism doctrine.

[35] The story has now become part of the fabric of early church folklore that Constantine saw a vision in the afternoon sky: a bright cross with the words: "By this sign conquer." As legend has it, Christ himself told Constantine in a dream to take the cross into battle as his standard. When he awoke early the next morning, the young commander obeyed the message and ordered his soldiers to mark their shields with the now famous Chi-Rho symbol. ☧

made the full circle from a persecuted minority to a favored majority. A short sixty-seven years later in 380, Christianity became the official religion of the Empire under Emperor Theodosius.

Constantine granted tax exemption to Christian churches as well as special privileges, such as access to the Roman Imperial system of communication or "post," which in turn enhanced communication between the various congregations. It also had the effect of hastening evangelization within the Roman empire.

By the time of the ecumenical council in Nicea, Constantine had assumed the role of arbiter of disputes within the churches over doctrinal differences, most particularly Arianism. At the Nicene Council in A.D. 320 he is deferred to by the bishops as the imperial head of the church, thus ushering in a sort of blending of imperial rule and spiritual rule—or, as we call this in modern terms, "church and state."

With the move of the capital of Rome to Constantinople (modern-day Istanbul), a distinct byzantine culture infiltrated the church. Still, heresies and doctrinal divisions reigned supreme over the interpretation of Scripture and doctrinal positions regarding the Trinity and the divinity of Christ. Following the death of Constantine and the sack of Rome in A.D. 410, imperial Rome disintegrated. Subsequently, doctrinal purists within the early church struggled to defend the apostles' doctrine against various heretical teachings such as Donatism and Arianism. Then, a single voice emerged on the scene to help in this struggle.

The Confessions of St. Augustine was a very personal and intimate autobiography written in A.D. 398. This treatise, which became a bedrock for Christian theology, shows the fluidity of the Christian faith during the fourth century.[36] Augustine's writings

---

[36] Augustine had himself converted from paganism to Manichaeism (belief that all matter is evil and spirit is good) to Platonism (a turning toward spiritual reality through mere reason and education) to Christianity and the

greatly influenced the medieval worldview, and his work, *City of God*, was closely identified with the segment of the early Church that adhered to the concept of the Trinity as defined by the Council of Nicaea and the Council of Constantinople.

The Medieval Church

During the Middle Ages, and the Great Schism of 1054, two distinct Christian churches emerged: the Orthodox Christian Church in the East and the Roman Catholic Church in the West. The regional wars that raged throughout Europe during this period played an important role in Christianity's dominance. Such pivotal points as the conquests conducted by Clovis as the leader of the Franks in 496 that led to the rise of Catholicism throughout Europe are beyond the scope of this book. Suffice it to say that the church had a predominant role in daily life throughout the Middle Ages. To this day, small villages checkered throughout France, Germany, and Italy often have elaborate cathedrals in the center of town that served as the source of civic and community activity.

In medieval Europe, the church and state were inextricably linked. As the Catholic Church straddled Europe for more than ten decades, all church government during this period was directed by papal authority.[37] And because the church exacted taxes in addition to tithes, its wealth and influence overshadowed any local attempts at autonomy within the church.

By A.D. 579, beginning with Pope Gregory I ("Gregory the Great"), the episcopal form of church government was firmly

---

concept of faith alone.

[37] In 1302 Pope Boniface issued the bull (papal law) Unam Sanctum, which stated that the pope had complete authority over not only the church but also over all the kings and rulers in the world. Salvation was dependent upon membership in the Catholic church and allegiance to the Pope.

fixed as the official structure of the church. Gregory laid the foundation for the elaborate papal machinery of church government. He took the first step toward papal control of the church outside of Italy by sending a mission of Benedictine monks to convert the pagan Anglo-Saxons. The pattern of church government Gregory established in England—bishops supervised by archbishops, and archbishops by the pope—became standard in the church.

Papal leadership in the church was eventually replaced by papal monarchy over the church. With this virtual absolute power, the power of the priesthood to make one's salvation conditional on allegiance to ecclesiastical authority, even in temporal matters, led inevitably to corrupt practices. This corruption was self-perpetuating and spawned by the stringent financial measures (*e.g.,* sale of indulgences, benefices, etc.) needed to support the growing army of clerical bureaucrats at Rome. The stage was set for a challenge from within the church to end the tyrannical control of the Catholic Church over the believer's gift of grace and freedom in Christ. Luther's *Ninety-five Theses* were the beginning point of a new era in church government.

7

Luther and the Influence
of Calvinism on Church
Leadership and Government

MARTIN LUTHER HAS BEEN DESCRIBED as the reluctant revolutionary.[38] The date often given as the beginning of the Reformation is October 13, 1517, and the reason often cited is that this is the date on which an obscure Augustinian monk, Martin Luther, nailed his *Ninety-five Theses* to the door of the Castle Church in Wittenberg, Germany. The Theses condemned greed and worldliness in the church as abuse and demanded a formal theological explanation from Rome on what spiritual benefits were bestowed by paying indulgences. The *Ninety-five Theses* were quickly translated into German, widely copied, printed and disseminated. With the recent advent of the printing press, within two weeks they had spread throughout Germany and within two months throughout all of Europe.[39]

From a church government standpoint, Luther stood to incur the ultimate sanction as his punishment for daring to challenge the

---

[38] Luther himself is said to have remarked: "I would never have thought that such a storm would rise from Rome over one simple scrap of paper . . . " Smith, *The Life and Letters of Martin Luther*, P. Smith (1911), 43–44.

[39] Among the more interesting of Luther's challenges to papal authority were: 1) the exclusion of the laity from control of the church; 2) the exclusive right of the Roman clergy to interpret the Scriptures, and 3) the exclusive right of Rome to call a council.

authority of the church. Rome used the threat of excommunication as a powerful weapon to suppress dissension and to keep followers in line with the code of conducts set by the church hierarchy. The Church taught that "it alone" was God's instrument and representative on Earth, and salvation could only be found by its means. Further, the Pope, as the leader of the Catholic Church, was by then declared as the "Vicar of Christ," or his personal representative.

Luther's challenge to papal authority was not merely a surface dissatisfaction with widespread clerical abuses; it was also based on a comprehensive framework underlying his theological understanding of the nature of God and divine government. This doctrine would later come to be known as Martin Luther's doctrine of the two kingdoms.[40] According to Luther's doctrine, the realm of appearances was very different from the realm of spiritual realities. He taught that Christ reigns mysteriously and invisibly over the spiritual kingdom, and no human authority can claim without justification that they are mediator(s) of this rule. It is by faith alone that we participate in this kingdom, and we must not be deceived into confusing it with external works or rituals. Similarly, Christ rules the temporal kingdom through

---

[40] To understand Luther on politics, we must know what he means by his doctrine of the "two kingdoms." The earthly kingdom refers to all rule or governance on the earth, or any government that could legitimately make use of coercive authority. This earthly kingdom included courts of law, and the political or governmental aspect of Catholic Church. In short, anything that had earthly laws which could force compliance and punish those who disobeyed could be described as an aspect of the earthly kingdom. The spiritual kingdom, on the other hand, was God's jurisdiction over the human soul and was concerned with heavenly or spiritual goals. Luther taught that this latter kingdom was free from all law. It was, instead, the reign of Christ through His Spirit in the heart of all believers. This spiritual kingdom could never be equated with an earthly magistrate, nor even the institutional church as such. It was truly "not of this world. Martin Luther, *On Secular Authority, Luther's Works*, Volume 3, (Ages Digital Library, ed. J. J. Schindel, 1997), p. 185.

His ministers of the law. (Romans 13). This same "two kingdoms" doctrine later adopted by John Calvin and wove its way into a foundational teaching of Reformed theology.[41]

Pope Leo X tried at first to simply ignore Luther's protest by dismissing it as the rumblings of a drunkard German monk. He soon realized that it could not be ignored, so he commissioned a professor to investigate the challenge to papal infallibility. Following Luther's later trial in May 1521, at the Diet of Worms, he was excommunicated and narrowly escaped arrest.

Local congregations in Germany celebrated Luther's courageous stand against the tyrannical abuses of the church. Province by province, they began throwing off the yoke of Catholic control. German nobles insisted in a letter to Rome insisting that they be allowed to choose their own religion. Their letter of "protest" is the origin of the term *Protestant*.

The Protestant Reformation quickly spread from Germany throughout the Holy Roman Empire. With it again came sources of contention over the form of church government and adherence to various ordinances and sacraments of the Church. Lutherans, for example, still adhered to the literal transubstantiation of the bread and the wine as the literal body and blood of Christ. Huldreich Zwingli converted much of Switzerland to his Reformed Church, but rejected the Catholic teaching on the sacrament of the Eucharist, forcing a break in fellowship with Lutherans.

John Calvin became an influential teacher of Protestant Reform theology in France and later Geneva. From his base in Switzerland, Calvin's church became a sending ground for preachers who would spread Protestant churches all across Northern Europe. That included John Knox, who founded Presbyterianism in Scotland.

---

[41] See, generally, John Witte, Jr., *Law and Protestantism* (Cambridge University Press, 2009); William F. Wright, *Martin Luther's Understanding of God's Two Kingdoms* (Baker Academic Press, 2010).

The Reformation Revolution in Church Government

The Reformation had a profound impact on church government. Shedding the hierarchy of the Roman Catholic Church was both liberating and challenging. For the first time in a thousand years, churches were presented free choice regarding the form and method of self-governance. Subsequently, a vacuum was created in church leadership. The episcopal hierarchy of the Catholic Church and its claim to apostolic succession of the bishopric was scrutinized by those who led the Reformation, particularly Luther, Calvin, Knox, and Zwingli.

In France, John Calvin, originally trained as a lawyer and later as clergy, published a four-part treatise in 1536 called *The Institutes of the Christian Religion* and intended as an "aid for those who desire to be instructed in the doctrine of salvation." The fourth *Institutes* book is a discussion of Calvin's view of the Church in Scripture. Whereas Luther left the subject of church government as a contingency of history, Calvin emphasized a return to the scriptural model of church government and pointed, as his source, to the book of Acts.

Alister McGrath, in his book *A Life of John Calvin*, states:

> Whereas Luther regarded the organization of the church as a matter of historical contingency, not requiring theological prescription, Calvin held that a definite pattern of church government was prescribed by Scripture. Curiously, the lists of ecclesiastical offices (IV, iii.3; IV, iii.4; IV, iv.1) which Calvin presents within the Institutes [of the Christian Religion] do not harmonize, and leave both the status of elders (or presbyters) and the number of ministries in some doubt. [42]

Calvin recognized that one of the primary purposes of calling out a recognized leader within the church was to quell dissension

[42] Alister McGrath, *A Life of John Calvin* (Hoboken, NJ: Blackwell Publishers, Ltd., 1990).

within the church. However, he admonished that such leaders should remain humble in carrying out their overseer duties, and not "lord" over those whose care they had been entrusted:

> All those to whom the office of teaching was enjoined they [the ancient church] called in order that dissensions might not arise (as commonly happens) from equality of rank. Still, the bishop was not so much higher in honor and dignity as to have lordship over his colleagues. But the same functions that the consul has in the senate—to report on business, to request opinions, to preside over others in counseling, admonishing, and exhorting, to govern the whole action by his authority, and to carry out what was decreed by common decision—the bishop carried out in the assembly of presbyters. . . . [43]

> . . . Afterward, to remove seeds of dissensions, all oversight was committed to one person. Just as the presbyters, therefore, know that they are, according to the custom of the church, subject to him who presides, so the bishops recognize that they are superior to the presbyters more according to the custom of the church than by the Lord's actual arrangement, and that they ought to govern the church in co-operation with them. Jerome, however, tells us in another place what an ancient arrangement it was. For he says that at Alexandria from the time of the Evangelist Mark to that of Heraclas and Dionysius, the presbyters always elected one of their number and set him in a higher rank, calling him "bishop." [44]

This structure of church government was a radical departure from the rigid hierarchy imposed by Rome. Calvin's teachings were instrumental in providing a new framework for church leadership throughout Protestant circles in Switzerland and France. Calvin was also outspoken in his criticism of Catholic rituals, particularly those having no precedent in Scripture—such as beliefs

---

[43] *Institutes* at 4.4.1, pp. 1068–1069.

[44] *Institutes* at 1069–1070.

in purgatory, sainthood, hierarchy, and the pope's worldly kingdom. He regarded these as a mockery of God's grace and argued that tradition had supplanted the simplicity of the Gospel.

Calvin's writings and those of his contemporaries sparked a Protestant break with the Catholic Church by many in France (Hugenots) and England (under Henry VIII) and led to decades of religious wars.[45] In France, Protestants were granted a reprieve by the Edict of Nantes in 1598, under King Henry of Navarre. This was short-lived, however; on October 18, 1685, King Louis XIV revoked the Edict of Nantes, driving thousands of French protestants to flee France under intense persecution.[46]

As a protégé of John Calvin's in Geneva, John Knox rose to prominence in the Church of England as a clergyman after his exile from Scotland. With the rise of Mary Tudor (Bloody Mary) and the brief restoration of Catholicism in England, Knox moved to the continent to avoid prosecution and is credited with founding the Presbyterian movement.

Anabaptist Movement

Another branch of Protestantism was also gaining hold in the Netherlands, Switzerland, and Germany, involving the Anabaptists

---

[45] The Edict of Nantes was a promise of religious toleration. It was granted in 1598 to the French Protestants known as Huguenots after years of civil wars. The Calvinist Huguenots came into being around 1550 when preachers brought Bibles to France from Switzerland. The growth of this reform movement in Gallic lands was astonishingly rapid. Within five years the new church held its first synod. Within a century it boasted a million and a half adherents.

[46] A religious war began in France in 1562 and culminated with the St. Bartholomew Day Massacre. The massacre began on the night of August 23–24, 1572 (the eve of the feast of Bartholomew the Apostle), two days after the attempted assassination of Admiral Gaspard de Coligny, the military and political leader of the Huguenots. The slaughter spread throughout Paris and lasted several weeks, expanding outward to other urban centers and the countryside. Between 40,000 and 100,000 Huguenots were butchered in cold blood.

(from the Greek *ana*, meaning *again*). This movement was the ancestor of the modern Baptists, Mennonites, and Quakers. These followers of the Swiss reformer Zwingli rejected infant baptism as a blasphemous formality imposed by Catholic tradition and having no basis in Scripture. Like their Calvinist counterparts, the Anabaptists were subjected to intense persecution by Catholics and even Protestants alike. Only the pacifist branch of this movement, under the tutelage of Menno Simmons in Holland, managed to escape such persecution. Today, Mennonite followers of this sect still adhere to much of the same doctrines and practices begun in the sixteenth century.[47] Many Anabaptist teachings became influential contributions to the Reformation. In particular, the following five tenets which are widely regarded as Anabaptist distinctives, have been adopted in several mainline Protestant denominations:

Sola Scriptura—an insistence on biblical authority for certain practices in matters of church governance and worship.

Separation of Church and State—Anabaptists correctly saw the church as the assembly of the redeemed, antithetical to the world and sometimes antagonistic to society as a whole. For this reason, they advocated separation of church and state.

Freedom of Conscience—because of the Anabaptists' convictions about the role of the secular state, they believed that the ultimate remedy for heresy was excommunication. They steadfastly opposed the persecution that was so characteristic of their age. They denied that the state had a right to punish or execute anyone for religious beliefs or teachings. This was a revolutionary notion in the Reformation era.

Believers' Baptism—The anabaptists were the among the first to point out the lack of explicit biblical support for infant baptism.

Holiness of Life—Anabaptists gave much emphasis to spiritual

---

[47] See *The Hall of Church History: The Anabaptists*, www.spurgeon.org

experience, practical righteousness, and obedience to divine standards. They had no tolerance for those who claimed to be justified by faith while living unfaithful lives.

It is estimated that today there are more than 180 major protestant denominations worldwide, not counting the thousands of local, nondenominational churches that trace their origins back to the Protestant Reformation of the mid-sixteenth century.[48] While the doctrinal teachings, sacraments, and religious practices of these various denominations vary significantly, they may all be generally analyzed in terms of their internal church government structure using three models: episcopal, presbyterian, and congregational.

---

[48] There exists a substantial disagreement among religious commentators as to the actual number of Protestant denominations worldwide depending on the definition one uses for "denomination." Some put this number as high as 33,000. See, D. Barrett, G. Kurian, T. Johnson, *World Christian Encyclopedia : A Comparative Survey of Churches and Religions in the Modern World*, 2nd ed. (Oxford, England: Oxford University Press, 2001).

8

The Hierarchical Form
of Church Government

WHETHER A CHURCH IS HIERARCHICAL or congregational in its form of government is of critical importance when it comes to dealing with myriad legal issues affecting the internal operation of the church, the selection of church leaders, and the proper means for resolving intra-church disputes over property, imposition of church discipline, and the ability of the church to decide its mission and statement of beliefs.

One need not look far to discover reported court decisions, both current and dating back to the founding of this country, in which courts have grappled with internal divisions between local churches and their parent ecclesiastical bodies. Typical sources of such dissension include property disputes, clergy appointments, and doctrinal issues. Oftentimes, these cases turn on an assertion by one party or the other that the opposing side has "departed from the faith" and is no longer the "true church." As we shall see, these are troublesome areas for civil courts. Some basic constitutional principles place several intra-church disputes beyond the jurisdiction of civil courts to decide. This is a complex area of the law in which even experienced, trained jurists often have difficulty in balancing the need for litigation to resolve a church dispute with the competing demands of the First and Fourteenth Amendments.

A Working Definition of a Hierarchical Church

In the Church of the First Born case, discussed in chapter 2, a central issue was whether the church was hierarchical or congregational in its form of government. The evidence needed to decide this important issue was intractably interwoven with issues such as church membership, the doctrinal positions the church had adopted over the years, the role of the pastor, the sacraments of the church, and scriptural interpretation. These are areas that are off limits to civil courts as a matter of constitutional law under what is called the "doctrine of ecclesiastical abstention."

The Doctrine of Ecclesiastical Abstention

There is a saying in the practice of law that bad cases make bad law. This phrase is perhaps an oversimplification of the unfortunate tendency on the part of courts to sometimes issue a decision that reaches an extreme result in an attempt to compensate for a unique set of circumstances. The problem is our judicial system of case law is predicated on a doctrine dating back to English common law known as *stare decisis*[49], which means that court decisions set legal "precedents" that are applied in future cases turning on the same or similar issues. In the area of church law, many of these early precedents failed to take into account the unique and special place that religious freedom has when deciding matters that touch on religious doctrine, practice, or governance of a church.

The earliest cases, for which we have documented records, in which courts struggled with how to handle church disputes

---

[49] *Stare decisis* is Latin for "to stand by decided matters."

came from the birthplace of the Presbyterian faith—Scotland. Sometime before 1813, it is believed, the courts had not adopted any settled rule for adjudging disputes between factions of a church. Believing they were not equipped to decide purely ecclesiastical controversies, these early courts tended to avoid the issue or controversy between factions of a church. Instead, they simply referred every question involving such matters exclusively to the decision of the church itself. As you might expect, however, this "head in the sand" approach to these cases presented its own set of difficulties. Oftentimes the local church's decision varied from that of its parent church organization; for many years courts seemed to vacillate as their views in one case leaned more in favor of congregational independence and in another case toward ecclesiastical subordination to the hierarchical body.

These earlier decisions, many of which ruled in favor of the power of the local congregation to decide its fate, afforded an easy and simple rule for courts to follow. That was only true as long as the rule was applied to independent churches. When it came to be applied to churches that were organized as a part of larger bodies, however, it created more problems than it solved.

Then, in 1813, the Scotch Court of Session in Scotland was faced with a case in which a local church congregation was accused by its parent church of abandoning a doctrinal teaching of the church and thus was no longer entitled to control over the church property.[50] The court initially decided in favor of the local congregation. Then, after the parent church petitioned for the case to be reheard, the court reversed itself and found for the higher church association. On appeal, the case came before the English House of Lords, which rejected both holdings of the Scotch court and for the first time stated the following rule to be applied in all hierarchical church cases:

---

[50] The case is *Craigdallie v. Aikman*, 2 Bligh, 529; 1 Dow., 1 (1813).

That property conveyed for the use of a society for purposes of religious worship, is a trust, which is to be enforced for the purpose of maintaining that religious worship for which the property was devoted, and in the event of schism (the deed making no provision for such case), its uses are to be enforced, not in behalf of a majority of the congregation, nor yet exclusively in behalf of the party adhering to the general body, but in favor of that part of the society adhering to and maintaining the original principles upon which it was founded.

This principle of church law means simply that where there is a hierarchical body, such as the Presbyterian General Assembly, a Lutheran Synod, or a Methodist General Conference, local congregations hold any property in trust for the benefit of these superior ecclesiastical bodies, and may only hold such property so long as they adhere to the doctrinal beliefs and traditions on which the parent church was founded.

Fifty-eight years later, after the House of Lords' pragmatic ruling in *Craigdalle*, our own U.S. Supreme Court had the opportunity to weigh in on this topic of how civil courts should decide church controversies involving hierarchical churches.

The case originated in Louisville, Kentucky, and involved a church split that erupted during the Civil War over the question of whether to retain a sitting senior pastor at the Walnut Street Presbyterian Church.[51] The Presbyterian Synod favored keeping the

---

[51] On an historical note, several denominational splits over the issue of slavery occurred throughout the border states leading up to the Civil War. The Triennial Convention (so-called because it met every three years) was the first national Baptist denomination in the United States. It was formed in 1814 in Philadelphia, Pennsylvania. In a dispute over slavery and missions policy, Baptist churches in the South separated from the Triennial Convention and established the Southern Baptist Convention in 1845 in Augusta, Georgia. Presbyterian, Methodist, and Episcopal denominations all split during the period between 1844 and 1865 over the issue of slavery. It seems today anachronistic and illogical how followers of Christ could credibly argue biblical support for the institution of slavery. However, it is equally

pastor at the local church and took steps to appoint new elders in the church that would affirm its preference. This power play by the Synod offended a number of the local congregants. So they took action to adopt a new articles of faith and constitution rejecting the actions of the Synod. The Kentucky Court of Appeals agreed with the local congregation, finding that the Synod had abused its authority and acted in a tyrannical manner. The case was appealed to the United States Supreme Court, where, in the case of *Watson v. Jones*, 80 U.S. 679 (1871), the court reversed the Kentucky Court of Appeals' decision and enunciated for the first time a doctrine that has survived to present day. It serves as a restraint or limitation upon the jurisdiction of a civil court when called upon to decide matters involving church polity or doctrine.

The rule of ecclesiastical abstention provides that courts have no jurisdiction and do not pass upon questions of faith, religion, or conscience. Specifically, civil courts are prohibited "from resolving church property disputes on the basis of religious doctrine and practice," [52] and when resolving such disputes, must "defer to the resolution of issues of religious doctrine or polity by the highest court of a hierarchical church organization."[53] Our task here then is to determine whether this church property dispute may

---

inexplicable to many fundamentalists in the United States today that the issue of same-sex marriage is being touted by several mainstream denominations as nonantagonistic to the Holy Scriptures. As we discuss later, the issue of same-sex marriage promises to be as much, if not more, a source of modern-day dissension in churches across America as slavery was 150 years ago.

[52] *Jones v. Wolff*, 443 U.S. at 602, 99 S.Ct. 3020 (emphasis added).

[53] Id. (citing *Serbian East Orthodox Diocese v. Milivojevich*, 426 U.S. 696 at 724–25, (1976). At least one court has held that the ecclesiastical abstention doctrine should not be asserted as a subject matter jurisdictional bar, but rather courts instead should treat the doctrine as an affirmative defense that may be raised by a motion to dismiss for failure to state a claim upon which relief can be granted pursuant to Rule 12.02(6) of the Tennessee Rules of Civil Procedure. *Church of God in Christ, Inc. v. L. M. Haley Ministries*, Inc., 531 S.W.3d 146, 156 (Tenn. 2017).

be decided without resolving questions of religious doctrine, polity, or practice. If not, then the ecclesiastical abstention doctrine would function as a subject matter jurisdictional bar precluding our resolution of this property dispute. Religious organizations have the freedom "to decide for themselves, free from state interference, matters of church government as well as those of faith and doctrine." [54]

This jurisdictional restriction is firmly rooted in the First Amendment to the U.S. Constitution and is sometimes known as the church autonomy doctrine. The doctrine holds that civil courts cannot adjudicate disputes turning on church policy and administration or on religious doctrine and practice.

The ecclesiastical abstention doctrine also prohibits civil courts from deciding which individuals properly constitute the leadership of the church or which pastor has been properly appointed or removed.

"[T]he issue of who should comprise the leadership of the church, a question significantly broader and more all-encompassing than that of who should control the church property, involves a deeper foray into the thicket of religious belief and church policy than was necessary to resolve the property dispute" and "issues regarding minister employment are protected from court inquiry because such decisions necessarily involve questions of religious practice or governance." [55]

Neutral Principles of Law Approach

Although the ecclesiastical abstention doctrine severely restricts a court's jurisdiction, it does not prohibit courts from addressing

---

[54] *Kedroff v. St. Nicholas Cathedral of Russian Orthodox Church in N. Am.,* 344 U.S. 94, 116, 73 S.Ct. 143, 97 L.Ed. 120 (1952).

[55] *Avondale Church of Christ v. Merrill Lynch,* No. E2007-02335-COA-R3-CV, 2008 Tenn. App. LEXIS 650, at *25–26 (Tenn. Ct. App. Nov. 10, 2008).

every case that features a church dispute, such as a dispute over church property. In those cases, the doctrine requires that courts use "neutral principles of law" to resolve the property disputes.

In the later case of *Jones v. Wolf*, the Supreme Court held that there are certain "neutral principles" that a court may look to in order to resolve certain intrachurch conflicts. These may include, for example, a controlling state statute, language in a deed, provisions in a church charter or bylaws, or other clear and established church precedent for guidance.[56]

The question of whether a church controversy "touches upon a matter of church discipline" is a legal issue for the court to decide. The following are examples of the types of issues courts routinely abstain from deciding:

- The qualifications of membership or grounds for excommunication; [57]
- Doctrinal positions on baptism or salvation; [58]
- Qualifications for ordination of pastors, ministers or chaplains; [59]
- Status of priests, ministers, or clergy in the hierarchy of authority within a church; [60]
- Decisions whether to terminate those in clerical positions in the church; [61]

---

[56] *Jones v. Wolf*, 443 U.S. 595, 604 (1979).

[57] *Nance v. Busby*, 91 Tenn. 303, 18 S.W. 874 (1892); *Anderson v. Watchtower Bible & Tract Soc. of New York, Inc.*, M2004-01066-COA-R9CV, 2007 WL 161035 (Tenn. Ct. App. Jan. 19, 2007).

[58] *In re Roman Catholic Archbishop of Portland in Oregon*, 335 B.R. 842, 851 (Bankr. D. Or. 2005).

[59] *Gonzalez v. Roman Catholic Archbishop of Manila*, 280 U.S. 1, 16, 50 S. Ct. 5, 7, 74 L. Ed. 131 (1929).

[60] *Kaufmann v. Sheehan*, 707 F.2d 355, 358-9 (8th Cir.1983).

[61] Recently, the U.S. Supreme Court reaffirmed that a church has an absolute right to hire and fire ministers and, by necessity, investigate and punish

- Whether a church has violated its own internal policies when deciding matters of church discipline or employment.[62]

One of the best means of assuring that questions of acquisition, control, and disposition of property is settled and beyond judicial scrutiny is to make adequate provision in the church's constitution and bylaws regarding ownership and control over church property decisions.

---

ministers without judicial intervention. *Hosanna–Tabor Evangelical Lutheran Church and School v. EEOC*, --- U.S. ----, 132 S.Ct. 694, 181 L.Ed.2d 650 (2012). Writing for a unanimous court, Chief Justice John Roberts explained that "it is impermissible for the government to contradict a church's determination of who can act as its ministers." Id. at 697. He reiterated that religious organizations have the freedom from official interference for matters of church government as well as matters of faith and doctrine. The Court expressly recognized the ministerial exception (a narrower form of the ecclesiastical abstention doctrine) to employment discrimination claims under Title VII of the Civil Rights Act and other employment discrimination laws. *Id.* at 705–06.

[62] *Ginyard v. Church of God in Christ Kentucky First Jurisdiction, Inc.*, 3:13-CV-931-H, 2014 WL 1089625 (W.D. Ky. Mar. 14, 2014); *Kral v. Sisters of the Third Order Regular of St. Francis*, 746 F.2d 450 (8th Cir.1984) ("A claim of violation of the law of a hierarchical church, once rejected by the church's judicial authorities, is not subject to revision in the secular courts."); *Nunn v. Black*, 506 F.Supp. 444, 448 (W.D.Va.1981) (stating "the fact that local church may have departed arbitrarily from its established expulsion procedure in removing [dissident church members] was of no constitutional consequence"), aff'd 661 F.2d 925 (4th Cir.1981); *Simpson v. Wells Lamont Corp.*, 494 F.2d 490 (5th Cir.1974); *Burgess v. Rock Creek Baptist Church*, 734 F.Supp. 30 (D.D.C.1990).

9

The Episcopal Form
of Church Government

HIERARCHICAL CHURCHES FALL GENERALLY into two classifi-
cations: episcopal and presbyterian. While both involve a
system of governance that allow for appeals to a higher, external
ecclesiastical body for certain decisions, there are very important ecclesiological distinctions in their church polity based
primarily on differences over the emphasis on church tradition,
the role of the bishopric, and each denomination's perception
of New Testament model for church government.

The word *episcopos* in the Greek refers to *bishop*. As this word
appears in its various contexts in the New Testament, it is also syn-
onymous with *presbyter* or *elder* and generally denotes a church
leader.[63] While the meaning of these terms appear interchangeable
in the apostolic writings, the historical development of the office
of bishop as it came to exist in the early development of the
Catholic church is key to understanding the various forms of episcopal church government that exist today.

---

[63] Peter appealed to the "presbyters" of churches to "fulfill the office of
bishops with disinterested zeal" using these terms interchangeably. 1 Pet.
5:1–2. Similarly, Paul writing to Timothy described the qualifications of the
office of "bishop," but later in the same passage refers to these in leadership
as "presbyters." 1 Tim. 3:1–7, 17–19.

Central to this understanding of the episcopal form of government is the concept of the "historic episcopate" and the significance of church tradition in the evolution of the role of bishop from the patristic days through the time of the reformation. The Roman Catholic and Orthodox Christian churches base their episcopal hierarchy on the development of the office of bishop from that of an overseer of a single church (monarchical bishop) to a multichurch diocese. By AD 200, the bishop in major cities throughout the Roman Empire had acquired greater influence over the congregations under their authority. And from the second century on, church governance within the Roman Catholic Church was principally through bishops. For the Roman Catholic, Eastern Orthodox, and Anglo-Catholic denominations, the authority of the bishop is derived from the tenet of apostolic succession—the notion that there is an unbroken chain of episcopal ordination of bishops that may be traced back to Peter.

To quote from the late British theologian Dr. Peter Toon:

> Those churches which maintain the historical episcopate claim that their polity is based upon that which developed in the providential guidance of God from the apostolic age through the first few centuries of the Christian church. For them, this means that it is both wholly in accord with apostolic teaching and takes into account the practical results of the evangelization, church planting, and teaching of the apostles, their fellow workers, and their successors.[64]

The authority of the bishop under Roman Catholic, Orthodox, and most Anglican and Episcopalian forms of church polity is derived both from Scripture and traditional practices of the church. References in Hebrews 13:17 to "them that have rule over

---

[64] *Who Runs the Church?: 4 Views on Church Government* (Grand Rapids, MI: Zondervan, 2004), 24. Rev. Dr. Peter Toon is a former deacon and priest in the Church of England and was a member of Christ Church, Oxford. He holds a Doctor of Philosophy from Oxford University.

you" and in 1 Thessalonians 5:12 to them who "are over you in the Lord" and to "such as these" in 1 Corinthians 16:15 all convey an order of spiritual authority and duty of submission to those ordained in such positions of leadership.

Similarly, the threefold ministry of bishops, priests, and deacons as practiced by the Anglican Church has its underlying basis in Scripture.

According to Catholic and episcopal tradition, the bishop's duties as the third in the order of clergy include that of ordaining other bishops, priests, and deacons, and to serve as a final arbiter of the doctrines and teachings of the church.[65] The office of bishop, in both the Anglican and Catholic tradition, derives its ecclesiastical authority from apostolic succession.[66]

The second order of clergy in the episcopal form of government is the priest or *rector* as used in the Anglican church. The English word *priest* derives its etymology from the Greek *presbyteros* as used in certain scriptural passages in the New Testament. Priests are ordained and serve in the role of local oversight over a particular congregation. They are authorized to administer the sacraments of the church. In the Anglican and Catholic churches, only priests can officiate at Holy Communion and pronounce absolution and blessing in the name of Christ.

---

[65] Toon would prefer the use of the term "synodical" form of church government to episcopal. " . . . [T]he dioceses and provinces are governed by synods, and the parishes by vestries/local councils. Thus it is preferable to speak of synodical government rather than episcopal government. A synod consists of a house of bishops, a house of clergy (presbyters and deacons), and a house of laity. Major decisions—e.g., a change in rules for church marriages—have to be supported by all of these houses. In contrast, lower clergy and laity do not have the same full participation in church government in either the Orthodox or the Roman Catholic churches, where a synod consists only of bishops." (Id. at 24).

[66] The Roman Catholic Church does not officially recognize the bishops of the Anglican Communion as being in the line of true apostolic succession.

Typically, in all episcopal churches, only priests may perform marriages, baptize, and hear confession.

The deacon occupies the first order of clergy in the traditional episcopal form of church government. The word *deacon* is derived from the Greek *diakonos*. In Anglican tradition it describes one who is "set apart" as a servant to aid the priest and bishop. Historically, in Acts 6, the term was used to describe those ordained by the congregation in Jerusalem to distribute food to the widows so that the disciples could continue their focus on prayer and preaching of the Gospel.

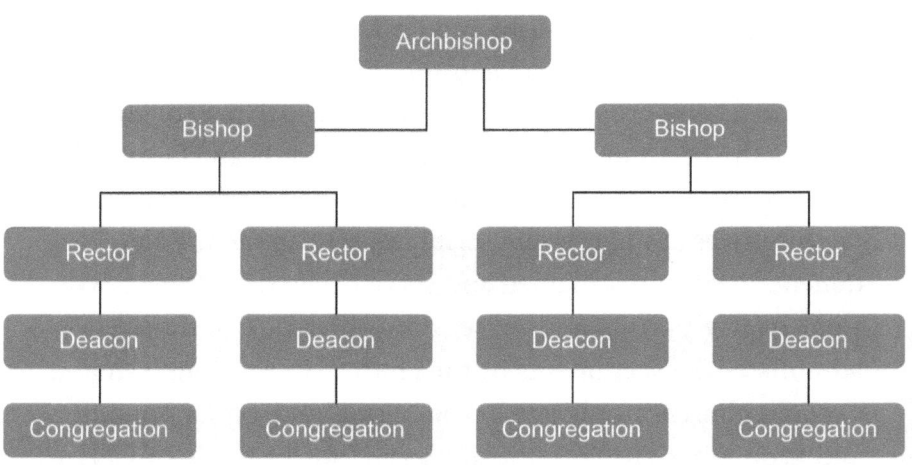

Today's episcopal form of church government is practiced by a wide variety of denominations including Catholic, Eastern Orthodox, Greek Orthodox, Anglican, Episcopal, Methodist, Lutheran, and others. This hierarchical system of church polity, which dates back to St. Ignatius, has many benefits, principal among which is an orderly process for resolving internal church conflicts.

10

The Presbyterian Form of Church Government

THE PRESBYTERIAN MODEL OF CHURCH GOVERNMENT, while hierarchical in the sense that the local church is interdependent and connected with other churches, does not vest plenary authority in a bishop. Most Presbyterian churches may be described as "conciliar" in their form of church polity, meaning they are governed by a council of elders elected by the congregation.

Presbyterianism traces its origins to the earliest beginnings of the Protestant Reformation and to its founder, John Calvin, in Geneva. John Knox, a contemporary of Calvin, introduced this brand of Protestantism to Scotland in 1560, starting the Scottish Reformed Presbyterian Church.

There is ample biblical support for a system of church government based on a plural-elder approach, as contrasted to the single-elder approach practiced by independent, congregational churches. As one early Presbyterian author and minister, David King, states in defense of this form of church polity:

> Since the appointment of presbyters in the Christian church entirely corresponded with that of presbyters in the Jewish synagogue, so we may conclude, that if a plurality of elders

stood at the head of the synagogue, the same was the case with the first Christian church.

. . .

We read of elders in each of the churches in Jerusalem, Ephesus, and Philippi. Paul, in addressing the Hebrews, says: "Obey them that have rule over you" (Hebrews 13:17). James exhorts him who is sick to "call for the elders of the church." These are individual cases; but we have more comprehensive examples on record. Paul says to Titus, "For this cause left I thee in Crete, that thou shouldest set in order the things that are wanting, and ordain elders in every city, as I had appointed thee. (Titus 1:5). Nor is this the only instance where such comprehensive language occurs. We read of Paul and Barnabas, that "they ordained elders in every church." Here, it is not said "in every city" but "in every church" (Acts 14:23).[67]

The Presbyterian model of a ruling council of elders also differentiates between *ruling* elders and *teaching* elders, at least within the traditional Scottish and Reformed Presbyterian branches of this denomination. While virtually all Presbyterian churches hold to the tradition that all elders should exercise a role as overseers in the superintendence of the church, most mainline Presbyterians differentiate between this pastoral role for those who are called or gifted in exhortation of Scripture and those who are not. All are ordained in a position of leadership as overseers, and, according to Paul are deserving of honor. "Let the elders that rule well be counted worthy of double honor, especially they who labor in word and doctrine" (I Tim. 5:17).

The traditional Calvinist Presbyterian model is also based on a democratic system of self-governance. The congregation elects its pastor as well as its teaching and ruling elders. This body of church leaders form, at the local level, what is called a "Session."

[67] Rev. David King, *An Exposition on the Defence of Presbyterian Form of Government*, 2nd Ed., Johnstone and Hunter (1854) at 124–25.

Members of the Session are elected to serve as representatives for a small geographic area, similar to a diocese in the episcopal system, on a church court known as the "Presbytery." Elders from these Presbyteries are then elected to serve on a "Synod," which serves a larger geographical area.

Finally, the church overarching body to which appeals may be made in questions involving church discipline and other limited issues is the General Assembly, which has jurisdiction over the entire denomination.

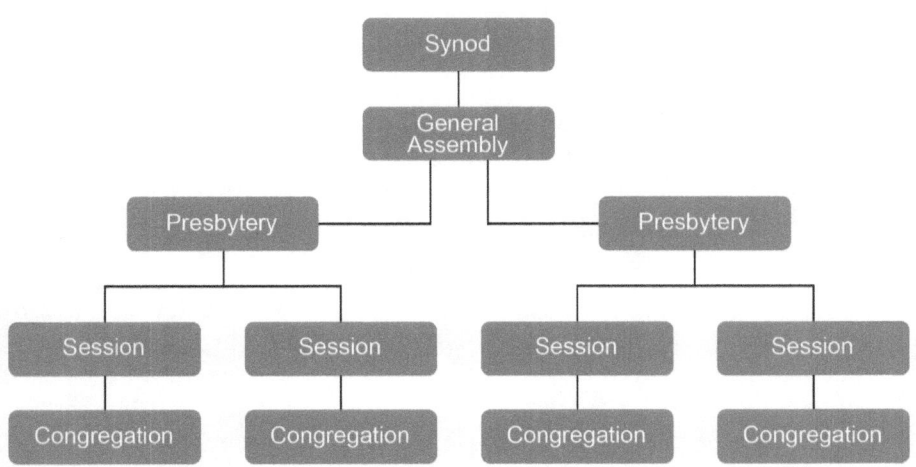

In contrast to the episcopal form, the flow of power in the Presbyterian system is from the top downward, with the higher ecclesiastical bodies having a very limited authority to resolve very specific appeals.

11

The Congregational Form of Church Government

Congregational churches are those in which each local body is self-governing and independent. The church is governed entirely in accordance with the authority it vests in its pastor (or overseer), board of elders/deacons, and its members. It is strictly independent of other ecclesiastical associations, and so far as church government is concerned, "owes no fealty or obligation to any higher authority." [68]

The vast majority of protestant churches worldwide operate under a congregational form of self-governance. Among those which practice this form of government, many argue that it is the one most closely aligned with the New Testament origins of the church. No doubt, the first church in Jerusalem began as an autonomous assembly of believers and functioned for several years under a purely congregational church polity. The apostles served as the initial elders of the first church, with James serving as the pastor. This internal leadership structure prevailed during the apostolic period until the early persecution of the church under Saul, when the congregants scattered abroad following the martyrdom of Stephen and the assassination of James.

---

[68] *Watson v. Jones*, 80 U.S. 679, 722 (1871).

In Acts we find two primary leadership offices, the apostles and the elders. In the earliest accounts of the Jerusalem church (Acts 1–8), the apostles essentially functioned as the first elders. Then the church scattered into other regions due to persecution brought on by Saul. But after Saul's miraculous conversion on the road to Damascus, the church of Jerusalem regrouped.[69] The first non-apostolic elders were appointed. Even though Paul and Barnabas were sent to Jerusalem to receive direction from the apostles and elders concerning the Gentiles, the Jerusalem elders were not in positions of oversight or authority over any of the newly formed churches in Asia Minor or Greece. Instead as churches were planted by Paul and Barnabas, they "appointed elders for them in every church." [70]

The modern congregational church movement traces its origins back to the Reformation era during the mid-sixteenth century. These were treacherous times for Christians who sought independence from state control and domination of the local church. Under the reign of Elizabeth I, church leaders in England during this time who dared to call together an assembly of believers and start their own congregational church risked criminal prosecution, imprisonment and, in some cases, the death penalty, for starting a church independent of the officially state-sanctioned Anglican Church.[71] Under the advent of Charles II, and the Act of Uniformity of 1662, some two thousand congregational ministers were ejected from their posts for denying the authority of the Church of England.

Despite this persecution, many so-called "Separatists" religious organizations stood firm on their biblical conviction that the New Testament church should not be subject to state control. Fueled by

---

[69] Acts 15.

[70] Acts 14:23.

[71] Three such Separatist leaders—John Greenwood, Henry Barrow, and John Penry—suffered martyrdom for their stand on congregationalism.

the writings of early protestant Cambridge theologian Robert Browne[72] and his contemporaries, such as Samuel Rutherford, these "Congregationalists," or "Puritans," as they were sometimes called, fled England to the Netherlands and the American colonies in search of refuge and liberty to practice their religious beliefs.[73]

In early eighteenth-century America, congregationalism witnessed a surge with the rise of Methodism and the Evangelical Revival in 1750–1815. Under the fiery preaching of evangelists such as George Whitfield and Gilbert Tennent, many were inspired to start independent and autonomous church congregations, and this form of church government flourished. These early American Congregationalists spanned a broad denominational and nondenominational spectrum of diversity from the Amish separatists who traced their roots to the Anabaptist leader Jakob Ammann to the Methodists under the leadership of John and Charles Wesley. The Philadelphia Baptist Association was founded in 1707 and began sending missionaries throughout colonial America to start congregational Baptist churches.[74] The so-called "Restoration Movement" during the Second Great Awakening of the early nineteenth century, under the leadership of Thomas and Alexander Campbell, Walter Scott, and Barton W. Stone, led to the founding of Churches of Christ. Campbell and his contemporaries abandoned their Presbyterian roots forming denominations under such names as "Church of Christ," "Christian Church," and "Disciples of Christ."

As congregational churches proliferated into the nineteenth century, they also grew in size and impact on their culture and in

---

[72] Browne was imprisoned more than thirty-two times as a consequence of his sermons and writings before being exiled from England.

[73] The *Mayflower Compact*, signed on November 11, 1620, was written by separatist Congregationalists (later called "Pilgrims") and was motivated by these same sentiments to break free of the yoke of Anglicanism.

[74] Samuel E. Waldron, *Baptist Roots in America* (Boonton, NJ: Simpson Publishing Company, 1991).

their local communities. One notable example is the Moody Church formed by Dwight L. Moody in 1858 in Chicago, which by 1860 had grown to more than one thousand congregants.

Today, congregational churches span a broad continuum of church government models and may vary significantly in their internal governing structure based on the following factors:

- The degree to which the church operates in a democratic fashion, with congregational approval as an essential component of decision-making;
- The degree of plenary authority vested in the pastor, overseer, or chief elder of the church, and the manner in which this person is selected or removed;
- The number and role of elders within the church and the spiritual authority vested in these church leaders;
- The role of deacons within the church;
- For larger congregations, the authority vested in "leadership teams" or ruling committees of the church.

Regardless of their particular form of congregational government, autonomy from an outside ecclesiastical body, and the ability to exercise self-rule certainly does not insulate congregational churches from internal strife and division. The measure of religious liberty afforded congregational churches in America today to flourish and practice their particular brand of Christianity stands in stark contrast to the persecution Christians suffered during the early post-Reformation. The greatest threat facing the congregational church today is not government persecution—at least for the time being—it is instead internal division from within the congregation itself. The best hedge of protection against this attack upon the congregational church is careful and deliberate attention to planning and preparation of the church organizational governing documents.

12

The Importance of Church Organizational Documents

W HEN IT COMES TO A STRUCTURE of church government, it is impossible to overemphasize the importance of a separate corporate entity as a legal framework for organization and a comprehensive set of church bylaws. As Rev. David King, a noted commentator on church government, once said:

> He is the Prince of Peace, and he promised peace to his people. But how could the societies of his worshippers be peacefully organised if the mode of organization were optional, and left to be determined by their own fallible and conflicting judgments? Under such conditions, discord would be inevitable. It is true that strifes about church government have actually arisen, and that no extent of privilege secures an imperfect discipleship against their occurrence. But the conflicts which result from the *neglect* of a standard are always more or less restrained, even while they last, by that standard; and they admit of eventual and satisfactory settlement. Whereas differences accruing from *want* of a standard have no moderating element and furnish no means either of prevention or of cure. Therefore, they must yield unavoidable and interminable troubles.[75]

---

[75] Rev. David King, *An Exposition on the Defence of Presbyterian Form of Government*, 2nd Ed. Rev. (1854) at 13.

The Need for a Nonprofit Corporate Structure

A corporate entity serves several important purposes in the legal protection of congregational churches. The best form of legal entity that offers the greatest protection for a congregational church is the nonprofit corporation. This is true for several reasons:

- It serves to shield individual church leaders from personal liability and those who conduct business transactions on behalf of the church from legal exposure;
- It provides a framework for identifying the decision-makers within the church, and defining their roles and scope of authority and accountability;
- Through carefully drafted bylaws or church constitution, the ministry goals and objectives, as well as the tenets and doctrines of the church, may be set forth with deliberate reference to their biblical foundation in Scripture;
- Conflict resolution is dealt with proactively;
- Church property and finances are better safeguarded and protected;
- Perpetual existence and organizational continuity.

Articles of Incorporation

The beginning point for incorporation is what most states refer to as the Articles of Incorporation, sometimes called a corporate charter. It is the foundational document that, once filed with the Secretary of State, becomes the official birth certificate of the formal church entity. While the information required in Articles of Incorporation may vary slightly from state to state, generally the following are required:

- The name of the church;
  The name and address of the registered agent;
- The name and address of the individuals incorporating

the church and who will serve on its initial board of directors;

- The complete address of the church's principal office;
- A statement that the corporation is not for profit;
- The purpose of the corporation, i.e. to share and defend the gospel of the Lord Jesus Christ in fulfillment of the Great Commission (Matthew 28:19–20);
- A statement that no part of the assets of the church will inure to the benefit, or be distributed to, its trustees, officers, or any private individual;
- The date on which the Articles of Incorporation were adopted.

As with any church organizational document, it is a good practice to incorporate citations to Scripture where appropriate. Such references demonstrate the supremacy of Scripture in all matters affecting the church. In addition, they underscore the uniqueness of the church from other nonprofit organizations and provide a theological basis for defending certain positions if ever challenged.

The Importance of Church Bylaws

Church bylaws are perhaps the most neglected and overlooked component of church governance. Many of the lawsuits in which I have represented churches over the years could have been attenuated or even avoided altogether had more attention been focused prelitigation on this important organizational step.

As discussed in chapter 6, to preserve religious liberty, untrammeled by state authority, courts limit their inquiry into church affairs and respect the boundaries set by the church in its rules of self-governance. It is not the function of courts to dictate a governing procedure for a church to follow. In a church dispute, the first document examined by courts is always the church by-laws. It is the beginning point for determining whether the church is "congregational" or "hierarchical."

The legal distinction between a congregational church and a hierarchical church is an important one, particularly in the context of an intrachurch dispute over ownership and control of real property. If a church is congregational and independent, its members constitute the highest authority on ecclesiastical matters, including church governance and discipline unless the church has specifically vested such authority in some other body within the church, such as elders or deacons or, in some cases, the senior pastor.[76]

Without a clear set of church bylaws, the lines of authority within a congregational church can become blurred. When internal dissension arises—as it inevitably does in all congregations—unless a proper mechanism exists for resolving conflict, the church can plunge into an irresolvable deadlock. Factions form within the church that disagree over the role or leadership of the pastor, the choice of music, the style of worship, whether to remove a church staff person or employee, and even the core doctrinal positions and practices of the church. The excuses for conflict are endless.

These internal conflicts can and often take the form of a *coup d'etat* to oust the pastor or some church leader. Tensions within the church can rise to a boiling point when a decision must be made whether to dismiss a staff member or youth pastor found to have committed sexual improprieties. Church members who have attended for generations in the church may harbor hurt feelings and resentment and feel that their tithes and offerings over

[76] *Convention of Protestant Episcopal Church in Diocese of Tennessee v. Rector, Wardens, & Vestrymen of St. Andrew's Parish*, No. M2010-01474-COA-R3CV, 2012 WL 1454846, at *14.

the years somehow entitle them to greater deference in church matters. Such deadlocks can be devastating to the church and lead to schisms that rip it apart. If litigation is filed by one side or the other, the controversy escalates exponentially. Precious time and resources that could otherwise be dedicated to the work of the kingdom is swallowed up in depositions, court hearings, and all the trappings that accompany a protracted court battle.

Recommended Elements of Church Bylaws

While it is impossible to anticipate all of the conflicts that may arise in the governance of the modern-day congregational church, the following are topics that should, at a minimum, be addressed in the church bylaws:

- Statement of Faith;
- Purpose and limitations for compliance with state laws and IRS regulations (no personal inurement);
- A final statement of the interpretation of Scripture;
- Stated compliance with the state nonprofit statute, such as number of directors, annual meeting, and notice of meeting directors and members (if applicable);
- Provision explaining membership, membership rescission, and member discipline;
- Provision about marriage, human sexuality;
- Job descriptions and limitations on employment;
- An arbitration provision;
- A membership agreement (not a provision but the acceptance of the church's offer of membership);
- School concerns (a statement extending the church's purpose to Christian day school education);

- A statement concerning indemnification of church officers and members;
- Indemnification;
- Terms of deacons and termination of deacons or elders;
- A web site URL to facility use;
- A catchall statement concerning authority;
- Statement that church membership does not vest property rights;
- Statement concerning who decides service times.

Church Law Institute regards its commitment to what it terms its "organizational initiative" to be among the most critical of all the services it provides to congregational churches. The importance Church Law Institute attaches to this initiative is borne out of the experience and lessons learned by Church Law Institute attorneys who have represented churches that found themselves lacking in this fundamental protection and who witnessed first-hand the devastation and destruction that followed as a result.

13

Governing the Congregational Church: A Biblical Leadership Model

ALL CONGREGATIONAL CHURCHES that are founded on the core, doctrinal belief in *solo gratia*—salvation as the gift of grace by faith in Jesus Christ—strive to enshrine Christ as the head and center stone of the church. Without exception, and regardless of their size, denomination or style of worship, all of the churches Church Law Institute has had the great privilege of serving uniformly agree that if the lordship of Christ means anything, it signifies that He is preeminent in all decisions affecting the polity and governance of the church. Obedience to His will is the foremost objective in all aspects of the operation of the church ministry. Certainly, at a spiritual and theological level, this central tenant must be true of any Christ-centered church.

Church governance thus becomes, in a real sense, the means by which this lordship of Christ is manifested within the local church body. As the church functions and ministers in Christ's name, it attempts to do so in submission to His presence through the Holy Spirit, and in adherence to Scripture. The structure of its ministries, the nature and function of its officers, and the relationships of its membership both within and without the fellowship are thus forms of expressions of Christ's governance over and among His people. As the church corporately submits herself to the lordship of Christ, the process, expression, and structure of this submission can take many forms. These span a continuum between a congregational vote being required for all church decisions on the one end, and a board of elders vested with broad decision-making authority on the other end. Church tension can exist when a local church adheres to either of these two extremes.

Without careful and proactive planning at the front end, a simplistic approach to congregational church government is often fraught with opportunities for deadlock between rival factions vying for authority. Without proper, biblically based mechanisms for resolving these tensions, they can erupt and cripple or destroy a ministry. Hence, autonomous, congregational churches are the most in need of sound, practical, legal guidance when it comes to a church government.

The best model for church government is one that balances the need for cohesion within the church as a unified church body, and the essential requirement of delegation within the church body of certain final decision-making authority. Such "authority" refers to that exercised over matters of spiritual leadership and the day-to-day operation of the ministry to those called to fill these positions of church leadership.

This model, sometimes called the "elder-led" model of congregational church governance is, we believe, grounded by scriptural precedence.

Scripture Verses on Elders and Deacons
Model of the Early Church

Now in those days, when the number of the disciples was multiplying, there arose a complaint against the Hebrews by the Hellenists, because their widows were neglected in the daily distribution. Then the twelve summoned the multitude of the disciples and said, "It is not desirable that we should leave the word of God and serve tables. Therefore, brethren, seek out from among you seven men of good reputation, full of the Holy Spirit and wisdom, whom we may appoint over this business; but we will give ourselves continually to prayer and to the ministry of the word."

And the saying pleased the whole multitude. And they chose Stephen, a man full of faith and the Holy Spirit, and Philip, Prochorus, Nicanor, Timon, Parmenas, and Nicolas, a prose-lyte from Antioch, whom they set before the apostles; and when they had prayed, they laid hands on them.

Then the word of God spread, and the number of the disciples multiplied greatly in Jerusalem, and a great many of the priests were obedient to the faith.[77]

Qualifications for Elders/Overseers

This is a faithful saying: If a man desires the position of a bishop, he desires a good work. A bishop then must be blameless, the husband of one wife, temperate, sober-minded, of good behavior, hospitable, able to teach; not given to wine, not violent, not greedy for money, but gentle, not quarrelsome, not covetous; one who rules his own house well, having his children in submission with all reverence (for if a man does not know how to rule his own house, how will he take care of the church of God?); not a novice, lest being puffed up with pride he fall into the same condemna-tion as the devil. Moreover he must have a good testimony among those who are outside, lest he fall into reproach and the snare of the devil.[78]

This is why I left you in Crete, so that you might put what remained into order, and appoint elders in every town as I directed you if anyone is above reproach, the husband of one

---

[77] Acts 6:1–7.

[78] 1 Tim. 3:1–7.

wife, and his children are believers and not open to the charge of debauchery or insubordination. For an overseer, as God's steward, must be above reproach. He must not be arrogant or quick-tempered or a drunkard or violent or greedy for gain, but hospitable, a lover of good, self-controlled, upright, holy, and disciplined. He must hold firm to the trustworthy word as taught, so that he may be able to give instruction in sound doctrine and also to rebuke those who contradict it.[79]

Qualifications for Deacons

Deacons likewise must be dignified, not double-tongued, not addicted to much wine, not greedy for dishonest gain. They must hold the mystery of the faith with a clear conscience. And let them also be tested first; then let them serve as deacons if they prove themselves blameless. Their wives likewise must be dignified, not slanderers, but sober-minded, faithful in all things. Let deacons each be the husband of one wife, managing their children and their own households well. For those who serve well as deacons gain a good standing for themselves and also great confidence in the faith that is in Christ Jesus.[80]

Elder-Rule

Let the elders who rule well be considered worthy of double honor, especially those who labor in preaching and teaching. For the Scripture says, "You shall not muzzle an ox when it treads out the grain," and, "The laborer deserves his wages." Do not admit a charge against an elder except on the evidence of two or three witnesses. As for those who persist in sin, rebuke them in the presence of all, so that the rest may stand in fear.[81]

So I exhort the elders among you, as a fellow elder and a

---

[79] Titus 1:5–9.

[80] 1 Tim. 3:8–13.

[81] 1 Tim. 5:17–20.

witness of the sufferings of Christ, as well as a partaker in the glory that is going to be revealed: shepherd the flock of God that is among you, exercising oversight, not under compulsion, but willingly, as God would have you; not for shameful gain, but eagerly; not domineering over those in your charge, but being examples to the flock. And when the chief Shepherd appears, you will receive the unfading crown of glory. Likewise, you who are younger, be subject to the elders. Clothe yourselves, all of you, with humility toward one another, for "God opposes the proud but gives grace to the humble." [82]

Pay careful attention to yourselves and to all the flock, in which the Holy Spirit has made you overseers, to care for the church of God, which he obtained with his own blood.[83]

We ask you, brothers, to respect those who labor among you and are over you in the Lord and admonish you, and to esteem them very highly in love because of their work. Be at peace among yourselves.[84]

After careful deliberation, and in furtherance of its commitment to fulfilling the organizational initiative for all its member churches, CLI has adopted as its exclusive recommendation to congregational churches a polity that follows an elder-led model of church governance. There are a number of reasons for this decision.

First and foremost, it is our belief that such a model best insulates the church from the risks of division inherent in a fully democratized form of church government. The single gravest threat to the institutional integrity of the congregational church is factionalization from within. When a congregation has thrust upon it decisions that turn on spiritual insight or which call for

---

[82] 1 Pet. 5:1–5.

[83] Acts 20:28.

[84] 1 Thess. 5:12, 13.

discretionary functions of church business operations, there are opportunities for division. That is not to say that the congregation—as a body—should have no decisional role in the ministry of the local church. Indeed, there are a number of scriptural references to support a churchwide, congregational vote on some key decisions such as: a) whether to impose church discipline; b) the selection or removal of an elder or overseer; c) the ratification of church bylaws; and d) the decision to welcome a newcomer into the family and join them in the covenantal relationship as fellow members.

Secondly, the elder-led model of church governance places the responsibility for the spiritual leadership of the church on the shoulders of those who are uniquely qualified—according to scriptural mandate—and who have ideally trained for this special calling.

Third, laying aside the absence of any biblical example of such church government, from a purely practical standpoint, vesting plenary authority for all decisions affecting the operation of the church ministry in the majority or super-majority of those members voting at any called meeting of the congregation is a cumbersome and ineffectual method of management. Questions can often arise concerning the validity of the vote or the eligibility of those participating in such an election.[85]

---

[85] Church Law Institute (CLI) respects the freedom of any congregation to choose its form of internal church government according to its own tradition and practices; however, for the foregoing reasons ,CLI has made it a matter of policy to respectfully decline an invitation to draft bylaws or governing documents which subjugate the church by vesting ultimate decision-making authority on all matters in the congregation.

14

Helping Churches Flourish

B EGINNING IN CHAPTER 4, THIS BOOK took a comprehensive look back at the history of church governance through the centuries, starting with first-century Jerusalem and the spark at Pentecost that gave birth to the church. Such hindsight is essential to any appreciation of church governance. But we often do so with tinted lenses overlooking the intense rivalries and heresies that plagued the early church as much as they continue to do so today. As Christians, we are not merely called to follow and support the teachings of Christ; we are also called to support the church, which is the embodiment of Christ in the world. John Stott perhaps said it best:

> First, I am assuming that we are all committed to the church. We are not only committed to Christ, we are also committed to the body of Christ. At least I hope so. I trust that none of my readers is that grotesque anomaly, an un-churched Christian. The New Testament knows nothing of such a person. For the church lies at the very center of the eternal purpose of God. It is not a divine afterthought. It is not an accident of history. On the contrary, the church is God's new community. For His purpose, conceived in past eternity, being worked out in history, and to be perfected in a future eternity, is not just

to save isolated individuals and so perpetuate our loneliness, but rather to build his church, that is, to call of the world a people for his own glory. Indeed, Christ died for us not only "to redeem us from all wickedness" but also "to purify for himself a people that are his very own, eager to do what is good." (Titus 2:14). So then, the reason why we are committed to the church is that God is so committed. True, we may be dissatisfied, even disillusioned, with some aspects of the institutional church. But still we are committed to Christ and his church.[86]

Through its Acts 6 Project, Church Law Institute is dedicated to providing carefully planned legal protection to churches, proactively helping them to avoid legal pitfalls that can easily devastate churches. Brian Schuette, an experienced church law attorney and founder of the Acts 6 Project, expertly represents churches in a variety of legal settings, both as counselor and litigator.

In addition, The Good Citizen Project is a ministry of Church Law Institute dedicated to transforming our communities, states, and nation through the power of the Gospel. Its founder, Joshua Hershberger, an ordained minister and attorney, is an author, frequent speaker, and lecturer at the national level in church pulpits, before state legislatures, and at church conferences.

The successes of these ministries far exceed the sacrifice in time and resources committed to these efforts, and the legacy CLI is building in bold, well-equipped churches and citizens is its true reward. We encourage our readers to learn more about this work and to contact CLI for more information on how you can support this ministry.

---

[86] John Stott, *The Living Church* (Nottingham, UK: InterVarsity Press, 2007), 19-20.

About the Author

L ARRY L. CRAIN IS AN ATTORNEY, frequent lecturer, and commentator who has litigated, debated, and practiced widely in the area of constitutional law and human rights. Crain's concern for First Amendment issues, particularly the rights of individuals to be free of religious discrimination, led him early in his legal career to serve as general counsel for the Rutherford Institute and later as senior counsel for the American Center for Law and Justice, where he litigated a broad spectrum of constitutional issues on a national level in cases heard before the United States Supreme Court; the Third, Fifth, Sixth, Seventh, and Ninth Circuit Courts of Appeal; the Supreme Court of Massachusetts; the Supreme Court of North Carolina; and the Supreme Court of Tennessee. He has also litigated at the trial court level complex free speech and religious liberty issues in more than twenty-six states.

Crain's legal victories in the area of constitutional law and civil rights have been the subject of numerous newspaper, magazine, and television profiles, ranging from CNN, *Inside Edition*, Fox News, the *New York Times*, *Washington Post*, *Good Morning America*, *ABC News*, and *NBC News* as well as several international newspapers. He has been the subject of three profile articles by *The Tennessean* for his accomplishments in the area of constitutional litigation.

Crain gained international renown for his representation of a Russian child in a celebrated case of child abandonment and neglect in which the adoptive mother in Tennessee returned her son to Russia with a note pinned to his backpack. In *Re Justin Hansen*, 2014 WL 3058439, at (Tenn. Ct. App. June 7, 2014).

In 2008, Crain won a million-dollar jury verdict against the Metropolitan Government of Nashville, Davidson County, Tennessee, for its discriminatory treatment of a Christian rehabilitation center in *Teen Challenge, International v. Metropolitan Government*, (M.D. Tenn. Case No. 03–07–0668).

Crain has lectured on constitutional law and religious liberty issues at the University of Strasbourg in France and also served as adjunct professor for law and religious studies at Moody Graduate School in Chicago.

He is admitted to practice in Tennessee, Virginia, and Washington, D.C.

In 2012, Crain's concern over the legal issues facing churches and religious ministries led him to form Church Law Institute, a nonprofit legal and educational ministry serving churches across the United States. Today, Church Law Institute, through its attorneys and its Acts 8 Project, is providing vital legal advice and services to churches in various states.

Born in 1955 in Tennessee, Larry L. Crain earned a bachelor of science degree from Vanderbilt University in 1976 and a Juris Doctorate degree from the Nashville School of Law in 1980. He is married to Florence Crain and has three children and seven grandchildren.